RIPON
HISTORY TOUR

ACKNOWLEDGEMENTS

Many people have assisted in gathering pictures and information for this book and its predecessor. Unfortunately it is not possible to mention all by name, but my thanks are no less sincere. I would particularly like to thank Peter Hills, Tony Moss-Blundell, Andrew Curtis, Fiona Turtle and my wife Dorothy for her unfailing support and encouragement. Thanks are also due to those, some of whom have since died, who have provided photographs or allowed access to images from their collections: Douglas Atkinson, Barry Drury, George Fossick and Ripon City Council, Peter Hills, Malcolm Hutchinson, North of England Newspapers Newsquest North-East Ltd, Mrs Richardson, Bill Robson, Tony Shepherd, Ian Stalker, Alan Stride and John Wimpress.

First published 2019

Amberley Publishing
The Hill, Stroud,
Gloucestershire, GL5 4EP
www.amberley-books.com

Copyright © Maurice Taylor, 2019
Map contains Ordnance Survey data
© Crown copyright and database right [2019]

The right of Maurice Taylor to be identified as the Author of this work has been asserted in accordance with the Copyrights, Designs and Patents Act 1988.

ISBN 978 1 4456 8915 9 (print)
ISBN 978 1 4456 8916 6 (ebook)

All rights reserved. No part of this book may be reprinted or reproduced or utilised in any form or by any electronic, mechanical or other means, now known or hereafter invented, including photocopying and recording, or in any information storage or retrieval system, without the permission in writing from the Publishers.

British Library Cataloguing in Publication Data.
A catalogue record for this book is available from the British Library.

Origination by Amberley Publishing.
Printed in Great Britain.

INTRODUCTION

Ripon is situated at 54.14° north, 1.52° west and 48 metres' elevation above the sea level on the western edge of the Vale of York, at the foot of Wensleydale, close to the confluence of the rivers Ure and Skell. Some 250 million years ago it was on the edge of the shallow Zechstein Sea, evidence of which can be seen at Quarry Moor.

Indicated partly by burials on Ailcey Hill, Anglo-Saxons had settled between the two rivers possibly as early as the sixth century. During the 650s the King of Northumbria founded a monastery of Celtic monks, with the famous St Cuthbert as guest-master.

Ownership passed to St Wilfrid in 660 under whose influence Ripon monastery became known throughout Europe, and his name has been honoured in the city ever since.

After destruction by the Danes and the Normans, in the second half of the twelfth century Roger, Archbishop of York, built a new minster at Ripon and laid out a market place and town centre, the basic plan of which survives today.

Ripon's economy developed with cattle and sheep fairs and cloth making and during the fifteenth century, with Boroughbridge, became a leading cloth producer. St Wilfrid's shrine put Ripon on the pilgrim trail, although at times this revenue was affected by plague and building catastrophes.

In the early twelfth century three hospital chapels were established: St John the Baptist's, St Mary Magdalen's (the leper chapel) and St Anne's. St Mary Magdalen's chapel survives and is Grade I listed.

The minster, with its chartered sanctuary, offered lifetime refuge to those fleeing the king's justice. Later cloth making moved to the industrial West Riding and during the Reformation the minster lost its revenues and canons. Catholic sympathy was strong in the area and an estimated 300 rebels were executed in Ripon following the Rising of the North in 1569.

In 1604 James I granted a new charter to the minster, restoring part of its endowments and establishing a dean and a chapter of canons. In the same year he granted a charter to the town, reorganising its government and creating the office of mayor.

Under the archbishops of York, a 'wakeman' had organised the parish officers including neatherd, pinder, swineherd, a hornblower to set the watch (curfew) and constables to patrol the streets. The 'setting of the watch' is still performed each evening at 9 p.m. in the Market Square. In 1617 James I passed through Ripon and was presented with a set of silver spurs from this flourishing trade.

By the eighteenth century John Aislabie of nearby Studley Royal generously supported the cost of the new obelisk, which his son, William, subsequently restored. Local communications improved: the main approach roads were turnpiked, a canal was built and regular stagecoach services were provided to Newcastle, Leeds and London. Horse and cattle fairs attracted rowdy gatherings, but polite society enjoyed a new racecourse, theatre and Assembly Rooms.

Horse racing started on High Common in 1717. There was one meeting a year and it likely included the earliest ladies' horse race in the country. It stopped in 1826 but restarted 'when a race course was formed and a stand erected on the north side of the river Yore'. Races were held here from 1837 until 1865, when a new course was laid out off Whitcliffe Lane, but that proved dangerous and in 1900 racing moved to its present site on Boroughbridge Road.

By the early 1800s Ripon was regarded as a large town with a population of around 3,000, and residential infill created overcrowded courts. From 1851 to 1901 the population increased from 6,000 to 8,000, resulting in significant building activity. By 2011 the population had reached 16,702 with a target of 20,000 to maintain prosperity.

In 1836 the minster church became the cathedral for the newly created diocese of Ripon and the town became a city. A bishop's palace was built. The diocese of Ripon was dissolved in April 2014 and incorporated into the new diocese of Leeds.

From the mid-nineteenth century, a railway, new hospital, new workhouse, training college for female teachers, new grammar school buildings and several primary schools appeared. Churches and chapels mushroomed and slums were cleared. Early in the twentieth century the Ripon Spa was created, but it quickly failed.

Ripon had close connections with the military throughout the twentieth century. Having hosted increasing numbers of territorial units in the first few years of the century, the city fathers applied to the government to establish a permanent army presence in the city. This was taken up at the outbreak of the First World War when a vast camp in four areas of the city – north and south camps, Ure Bank and the racecourse sites – was established. It could take two divisions, some 30,000 soldiers, and it is estimated that 350,000 passed through during the First World War. It was used for training, for convalescence (having a military hospital of 670 beds) and for prisoners of war.

At the start of the Second World War as Harper Barracks, it was used for engineering training and additionally in 1941 for the School of Bomb Disposal. During the 1950s the Royal Signals Training Regiment was based here.

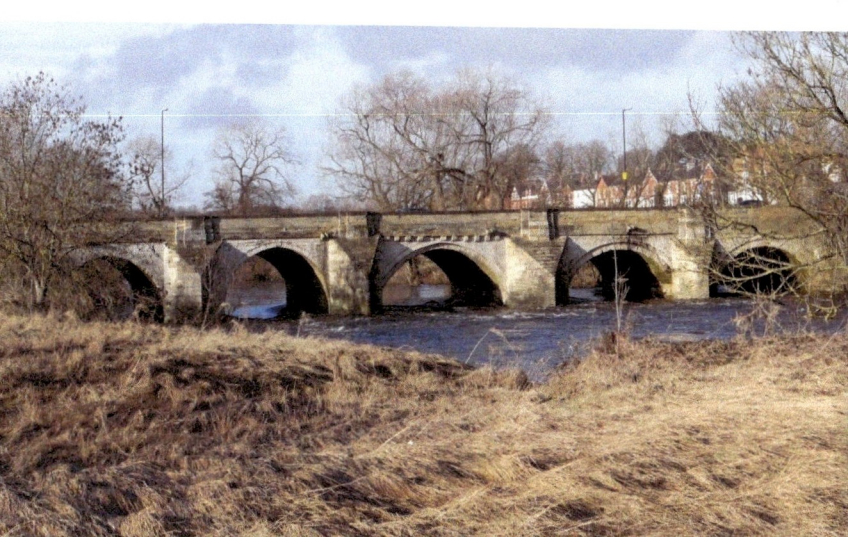

38 Engineering Regiment took over the site, which was rebuilt and renamed Claro Barracks from 1959 to 2008 when it transferred to 21 Engineer Regiment. In 2016 three years' notice of closure was announced.

The 1974 local government reorganisation reduced the city council to a parish council within the borough of Harrogate and brought the loss of the coveted 'city' title, although this was fortunately reinstated when the Queen graciously granted honorary city status.

One of many occasions during the twentieth century that the military paraded through the city, culminating in the Royal Engineers being granted the Freedom of the City in 1949 and an annual march past and service in the cathedral on Remembrance Sunday. In the picture above, taken in 1998–99, Mayor Barry Kay takes the salute as the Royal Engineers march past.

ARMS OF THE CITY OF RIPON

EXCEPT YE LORD KEEP YE
CITTIE, YE WAKEMAN WAKETH
IN VAIN.

feb. 9th 1905

PARKER, RIPON. Copyright.

The arms of the city of Ripon are seen here on a card purchased in 1905. Stephen Tucker, Rouge Croix of the College of Heralds, said he had 'not been able to make the banner an armorial one as Ripon is not, and never was, entitled to arms, and is, I believe, the only city in England so circumstanced'. The arms include the symbols of the horn of the claimed King Alfred charter and the famous Ripon rowel spurs from the seventeenth/eighteenth century.

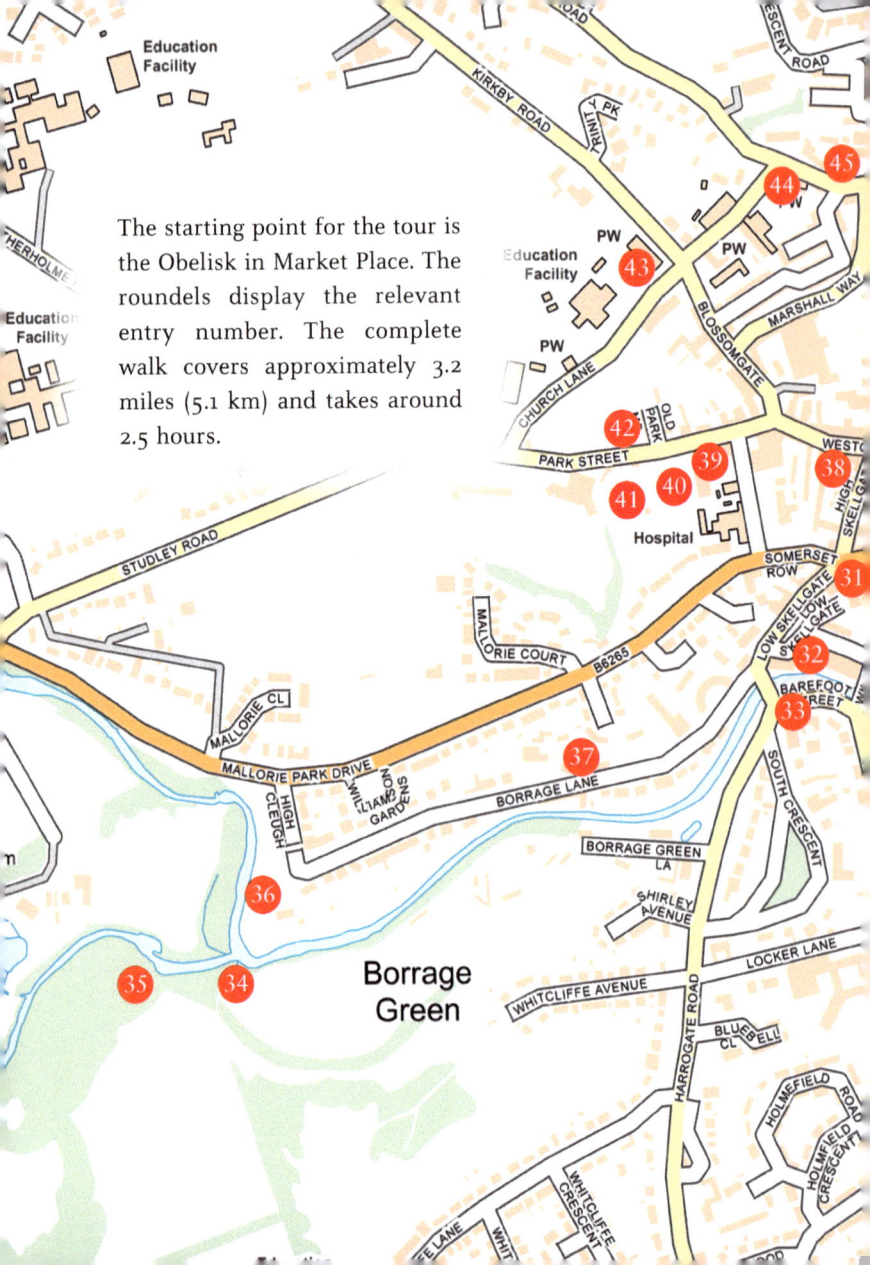

The starting point for the tour is the Obelisk in Market Place. The roundels display the relevant entry number. The complete walk covers approximately 3.2 miles (5.1 km) and takes around 2.5 hours.

RIPON

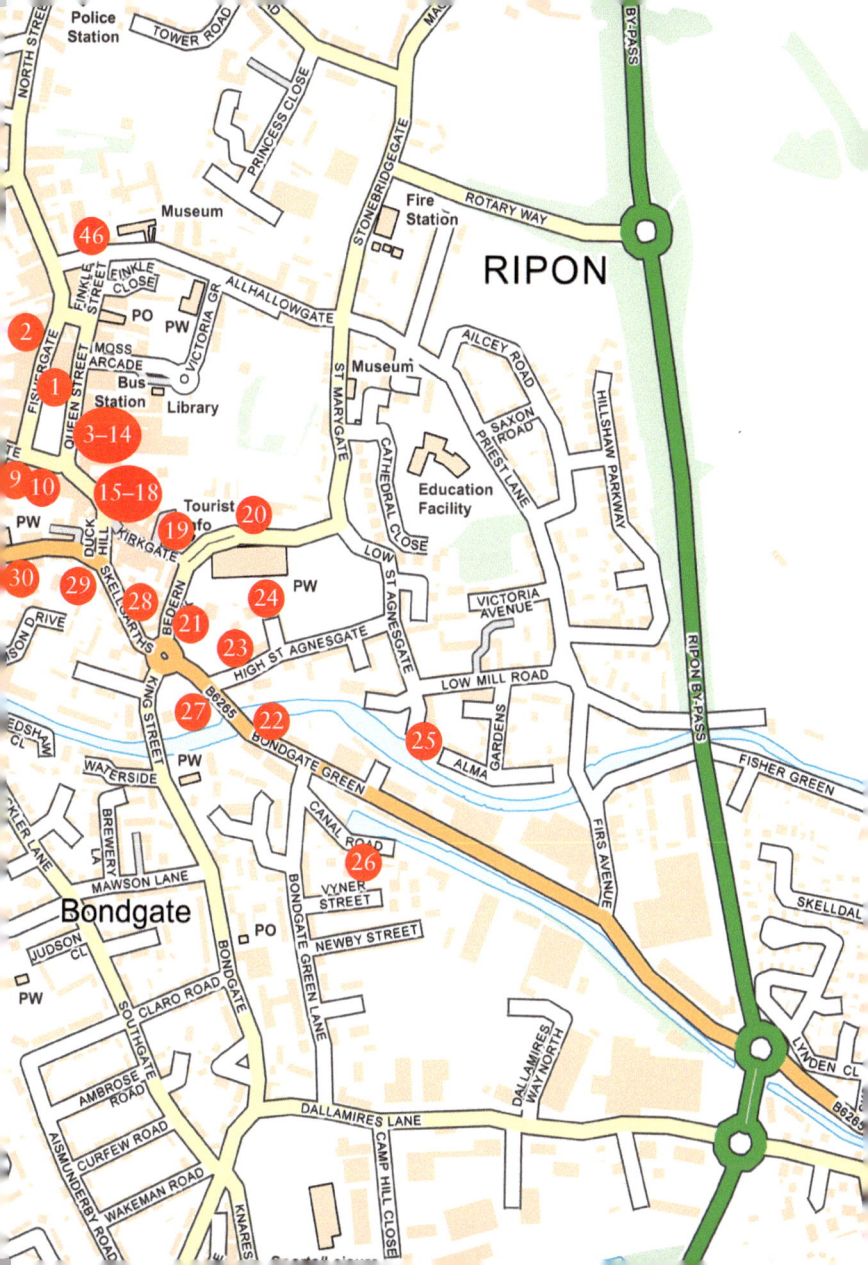

Police Station
Museum
Fire Station
Bus Station
Library
Museum
Education Facility
Tourist Info

Bondgate

Streets and roads: TOWER ROAD, NORTH STREET, PRINCESS CLOSE, STONEBRIDGEGATE, BY-PASS, ROTARY WAY, FINKLE STREET, FINKLE CLOSE, ALLHALLOWGATE, AILCEY ROAD, HILLSHAW PARKWAY, FISHERGATE, QUEEN STREET, MQSS ARCADE, VICTORIA GR, ST MARYGATE, SAXON ROAD, PRIEST LANE, RIPON BY-PASS, QUICK HILL, KIRKGATE, BEDERN, SKELLGARTHS, CATHEDRAL CLOSE, LOW ST AGNESGATE, VICTORIA AVENUE, HIGH ST AGNESGATE, LOW MILL ROAD, KING STREET, B6265, BONDGATE GREEN, ALMA GARDENS, FISHER GREEN, FIRS AVENUE, SKELLDAL, WATERSIDE, CANAL ROAD, BREWERY LA, MAWSON LANE, VYNER STREET, BONDGATE GREEN LANE, NEWBY STREET, JUDSON CL, CLARO ROAD, SOUTHGATE, BONDGATE, AMBROSE ROAD, CURFEW ROAD, AISMUNDERBY ROAD, WAKEMAN ROAD, KNARES, DALLAMIRES LANE, DALLAMIRES WAY NORTH, CAMP HILL CLOSE, LYNDEN CL

KEY

1. Market Place
2. Fishergate/Lavender Alley
3. Market Place
4. Market Day
5. Market Place
6. The Hornblower
7. The Bellman
8. Market Day just before the First World War
9. The Wakeman's House
10. Market Place and Westgate
11. Market Day
12. Unicorn Hotel (Wetherspoons)
13. Sainsbury's site
14. Market Place South
15. Kirkgate
16. Kirkgate
17. Kirkgate
18. Kirkgate
19. Ripon Cathedral West Front
20. The Old Deanery
21. The Cathedral from Bedern Bank
22. Bondgate Green Bridge
23. High St Agnesgate/St Anne's Hospital Chapel
24. Ripon Cathedral South Walk
25. Alma Weir and Footbridge
26. Canal Basin
27. Mill Field Play Park
28. Ripon Cathedral from York Yard
29. Duck Hill Mill
30. Water Skellgate
31. Low Skellgate
32. Williamson Paint Works and River Skell
33. Borrage Bridge
34. Rustic Bridge
35. Fairy Steps
36. High Cleugh
37. Borrage Lane
38. Westgate
39. Spa Baths
40. Spa Gardens
41. Spa Gardens Bandstand and Spa Hotel
42. Spa Park
43. Holy Trinity Church
44. St Wilfrid's Roman Catholic Church
45. Coltsgate Hill
46. North Street

1. MARKET PLACE

Since it was laid out under the orders of the Archbishop of York in the twelfth/thirteenth century, Ripon's commercial life has been focused on the Market Place, which provided the archbishop with a handsome income from rents, tolls and other dues, possibly also helping to fund the building of the new minster. When Daniel Defoe visited in 1726, he said it was 'the finest and most beautiful square that is to be seen of its kind in England'. The regular weekly market, seen here around 1894, typifies the fairs and markets held on the square for centuries. Note the unwidened entrance to Fishergate.

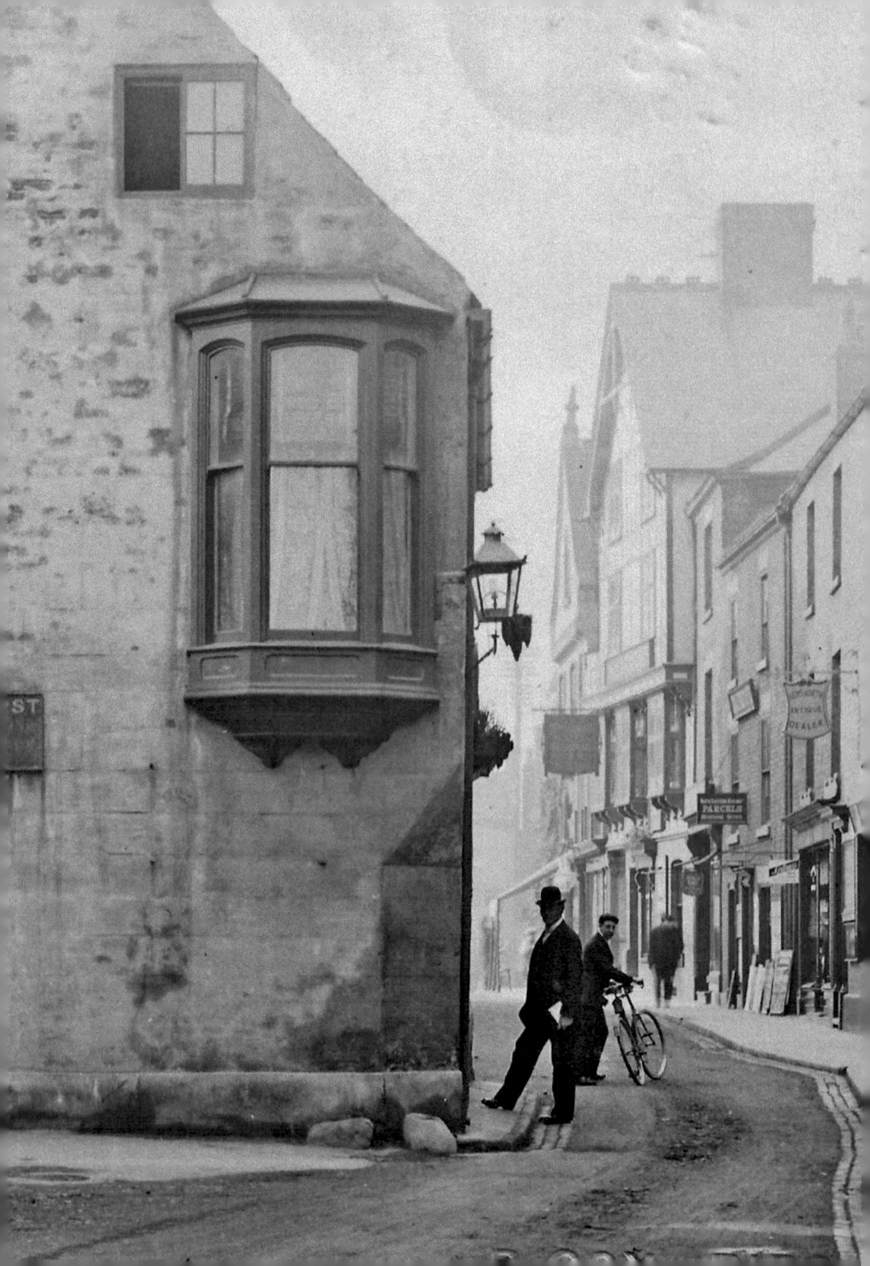
ST
ANTIQUE
DEALER
PARCELS

2. FISHERGATE/LAVENDER ALLEY

Leading north from the Market Place at the turn of the twentieth century, Fishergate's narrowness was causing concern. This 1906 view, looking south, shows it immediately prior to the demolition of its eastern (left) side and its width doubled. The Grapes Inn, at the corner of Lavender Alley, was the last building to go.

A charter, said to have been given in 1108 to 'Thomas, archbishop of York and St Wilfrid', refers to a weekly market and a four-day fair (animal sale) in April. As a result the Archbishop of York's officers not only collected tolls but checked the weights, tasted the ale, etc., and monitored the coinage. Offenders were brought before the court the same day. Penalties often involved time in the stocks or pillory.

Originally the Market Place covered a much larger area and in the centre stood the market cross with the tollbooth close by and the stocks, whipping post and gallows in its yard. This was probably where Lavender Alley is now. Executions would have taken place here until they were transferred to Gallows Hill in the sixteenth century, remaining there until 1723. Up to the 1830s most of those convicted at the quarter sessions were whipped at the market cross 'till their backs be bloody' or later fastened to the back of a cart and whipped with a cat-o'-nine-tails around the Market Place at two o'clock on market day.

Market Place.

3. MARKET PLACE

The visual impact of the Market Square stems from its size and spaciousness, especially when reached down narrow streets. Until late Victorian times the approaches were even narrower and, in the north-east corner, Middle Street halved the width of what is now Queen Street. From at least the twelfth century Thursday has been Ripon's market day and may be related to ancient celebrations marking the day St Wilfrid died.

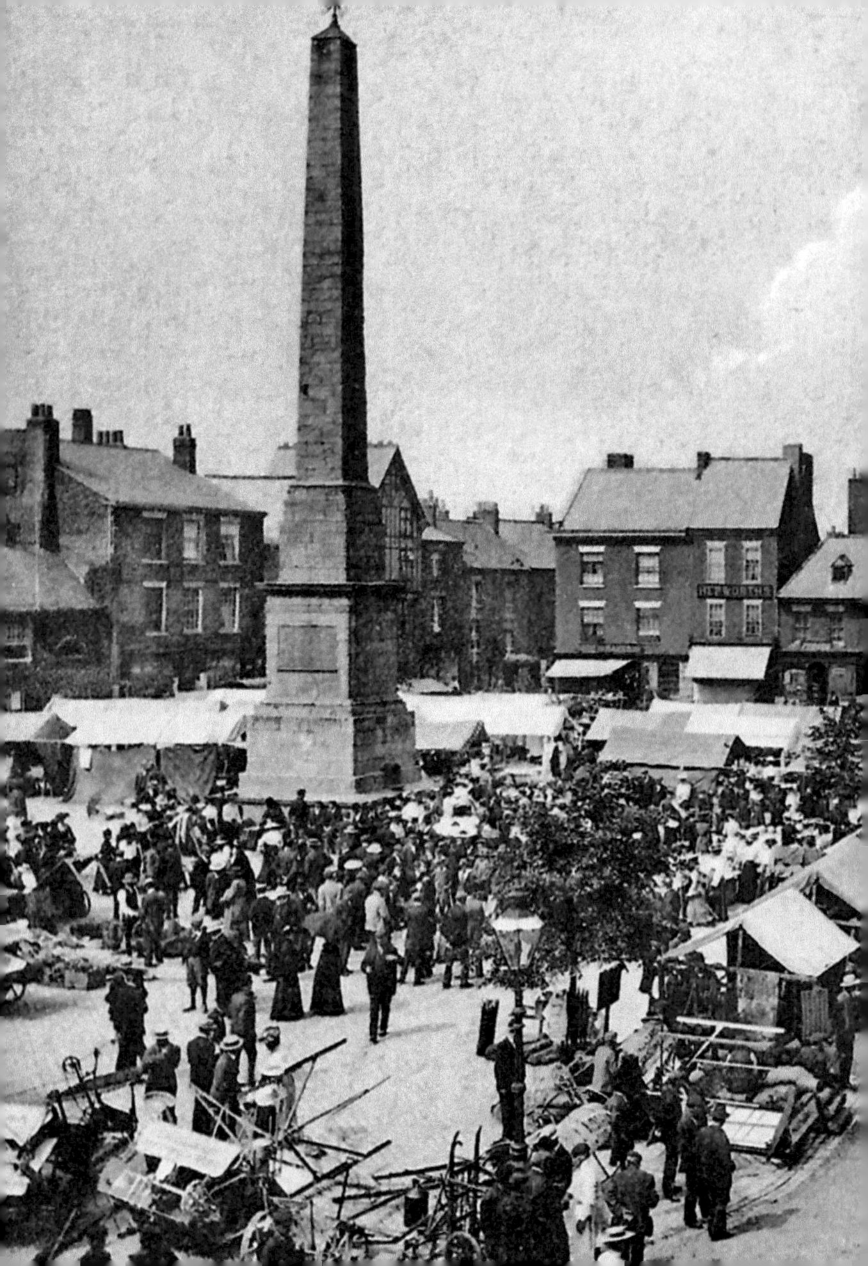

4. MARKET DAY

This card is postmarked November 1909 and shows the effect of the demolition, a year or two earlier, of Middle Street and the removal of one bay of the building, now Thomas's bakers, to widen Fishergate by some 3 metres. The burgage plots gave voting and grazing rights. The widths vary around multiples of 15 feet. The omnibus carried passengers between the Unicorn Hotel and the railway station at Ure Bank.

Market Place, Ripon.

5. MARKET PLACE

The focal point of the Market Place is undoubtedly the obelisk, part of a scheme designed by Nicholas Hawksmoor. The original was built in 1702 under John Aislabie of Studley Royal, then mayor of Ripon, and restored in 1781 by his son, William. The obelisk replaced an earlier market cross and Aislabie paid over half the cost, as well as providing the limestone from his quarries.

Standing 90 feet high, it is topped by a rowel spur and horn, symbols of Ripon's ancient crafts and customs, and was extensively restored in 1985. This card is postmarked 1903.

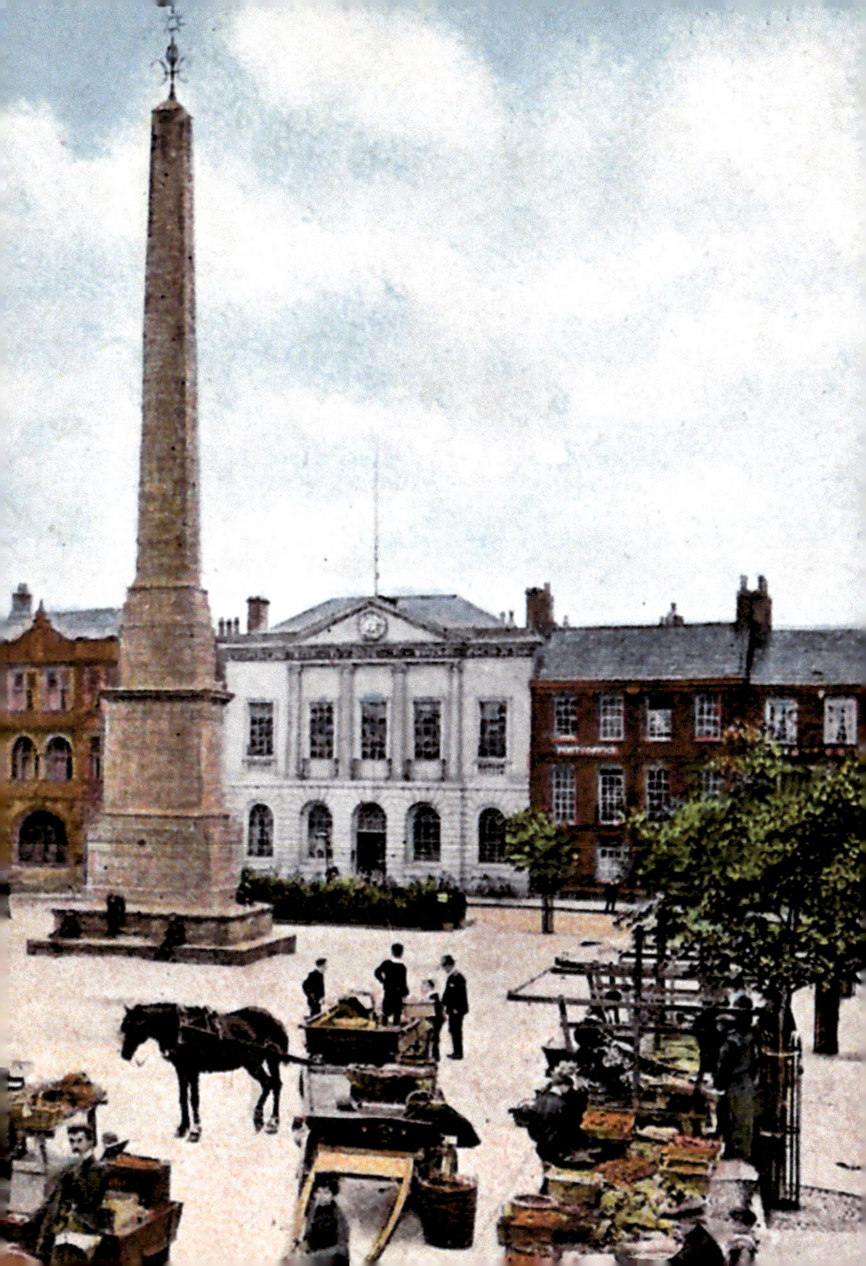

6. THE HORNBLOWER

Unique to Ripon, nightly at nine o'clock at the obelisk, the hornblower 'sets the watch'. This has possibly been happening from the setting out of the new Market Place in the thirteenth century. Initially the horn was blown first at the mayor's residence, then in the Market Place. That reversed in 1913 so visitors could catch the 9.29 p.m. train to Harrogate. When war was declared in 1939 the horn was blown at 6 p.m.; from 1941 this was changed to the start of blackout if earlier than 9 p.m.

7. THE BELLMAN

At 11 a.m. on Thursdays the bellman, whose office can be dated to before 1367, appears on the Market Square. The cornmarket, which he is opening, actually started at noon. The Corporation had the right to levy a toll – market sweepings – on each sack of corn sold. His other duties included making announcements, starting the quarter sessions and administering whippings, for which he was paid 5s. He would be sent to cry 'Cautions!' if a breach of the byelaws was suspected, and he read the Riot Act.

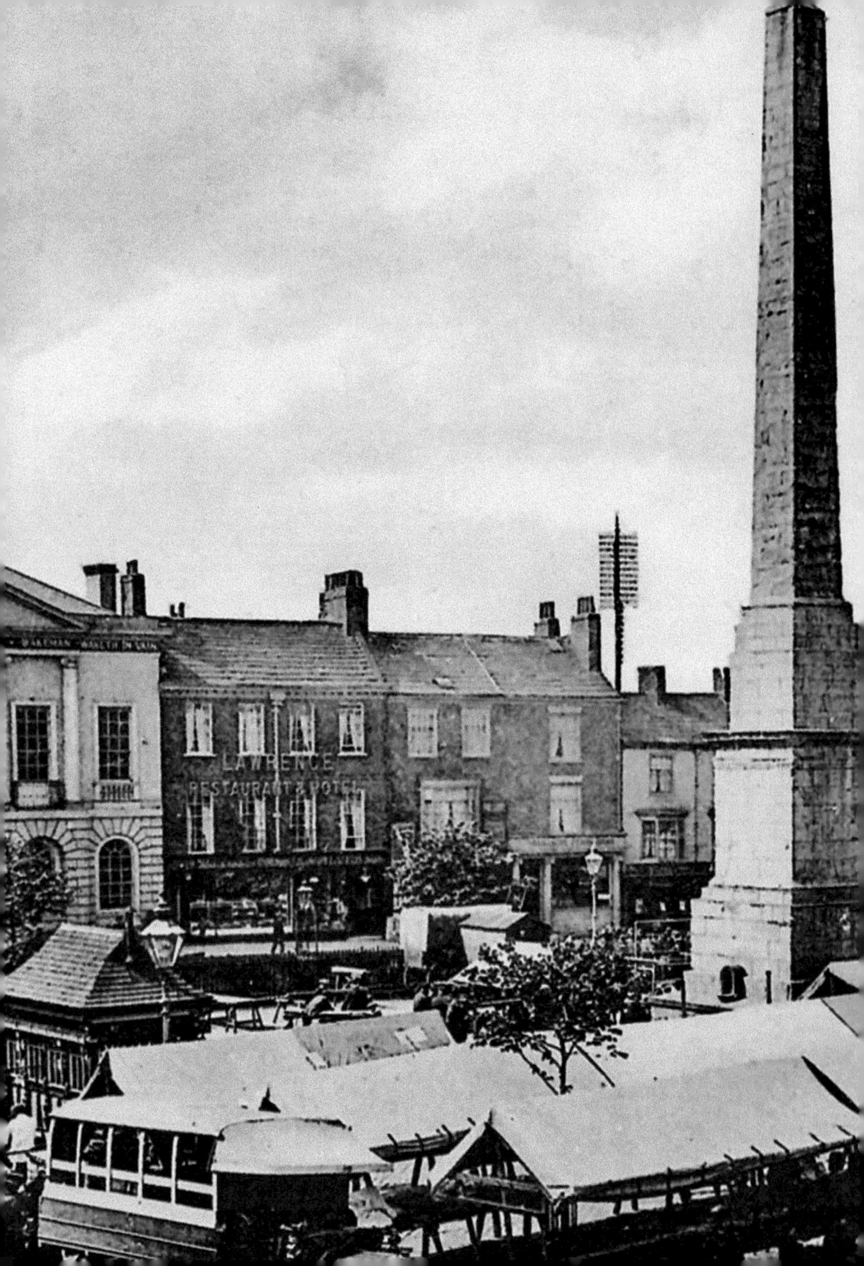
LAWRENCE
RESTAURANT & HOTEL

8. MARKET DAY JUST BEFORE THE FIRST WORLD WAR

Note that animal pens are back on the square. Beyond the motor bus the cabmen's shelter can be seen, provided in 1911 for local horse cab drivers by Miss Sarah Carter, daughter of a former mayor. In later years it fell into disuse, but in 1985 in view of its rarity, Ripon Civic Society undertook its restoration. The telegraph office, from 1869 at No. 35, can be picked out by the mast.

THE MEMORY OF
HUGH RIPLEY
WAKEFIELD'S FIRST MAYOR IS

PRECIOUS

9. THE WAKEMAN'S HOUSE

Once thought to have been the home of Hugh Ripley, the last Ripon wakeman, and threatened with demolition, the council bought the late medieval house in 1917 and added a wartime food kitchen, which was demolished in 2000 for public toilets. To its right, Thirlway's shop was demolished around 1940. After restoration the house became a local history museum, a café and the tourist information office. From 1990 it was occupied by Ripon Improvement Trust but has since reverted to being a café.

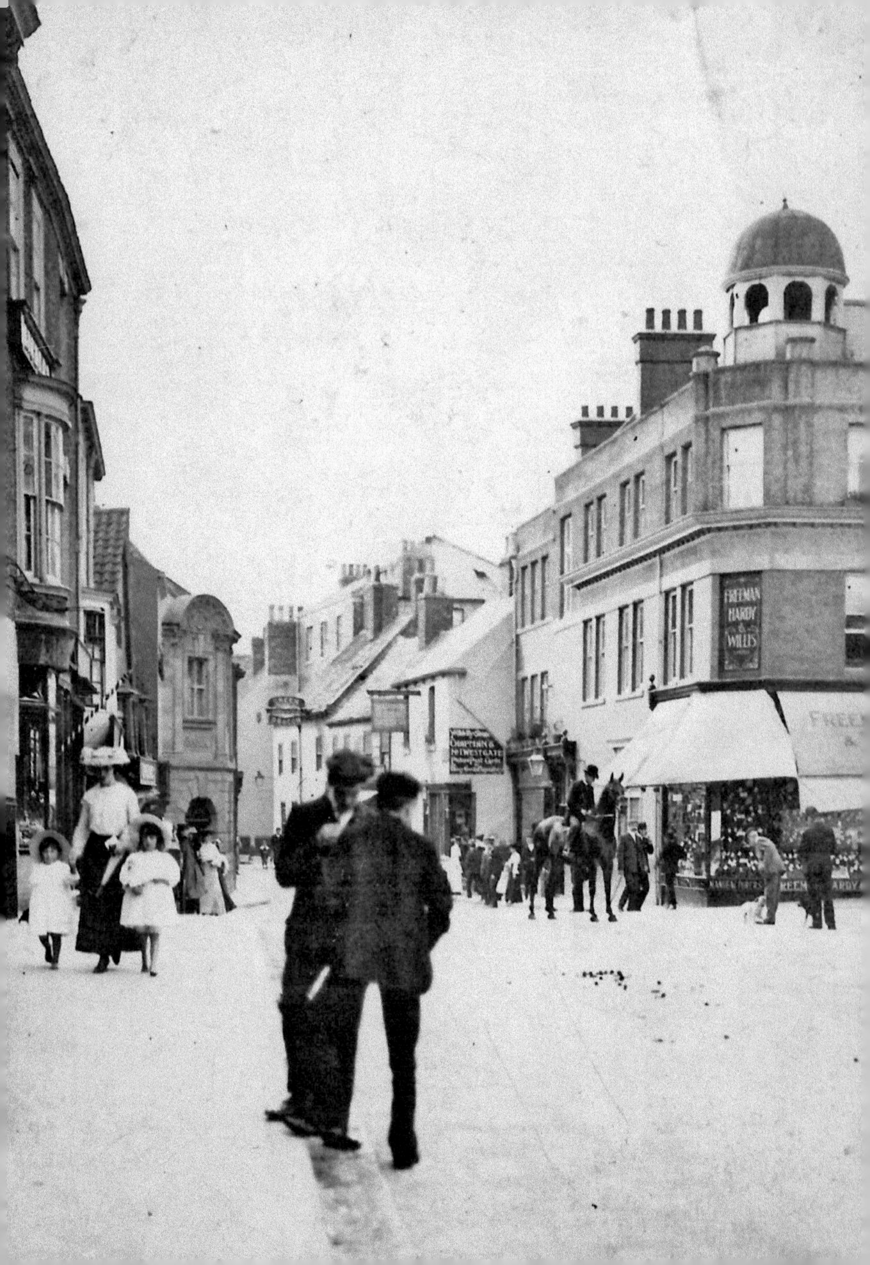
FREEMAN HARDY & WILLIS

10. MARKET PLACE AND WESTGATE

The building on the corner with its cupola, formerly Freeman Hardy and Willis, then Stead & Simpson and now the Yorkshire Building Society and a bank at the High Skellgate junction, are shown here in 1905. The cupola survived into the 1960s. The picture shows that Westgate's widening had begun, but the two pubs on the right – The Queen Alexandra and the Green Dragon – were still awaiting demolition. The scheme was never completed and the road narrows again.

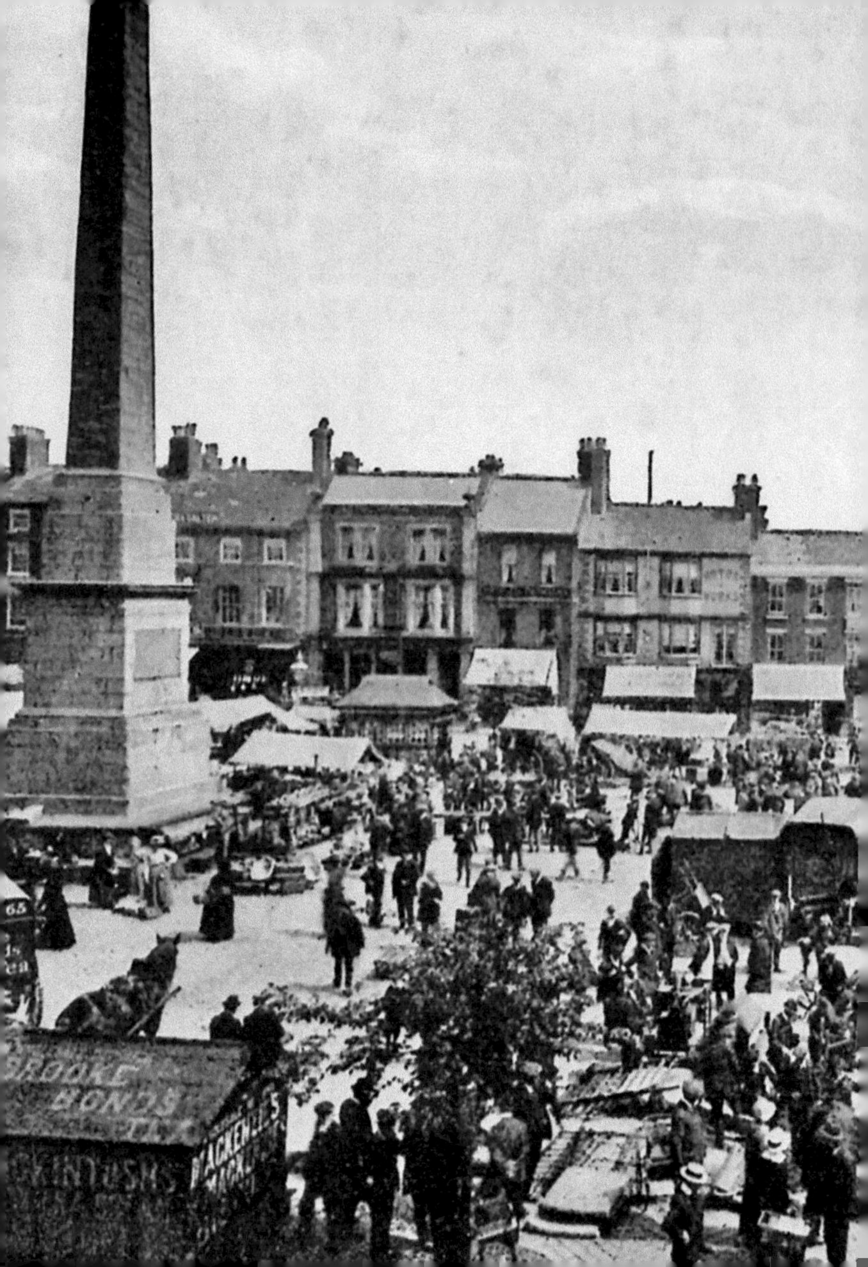
BONDS
65

11. MARKET DAY

A busy market around the time of the First World War, a time when cars were still rare. Croft and Blackburn's Motor Works arrived in 1908. The building on the corner of Kirkgate was demolished for road widening in 1931. The Skipton Building Society now occupies part of the site. Farmers gather at the south-west corner.

12. UNICORN HOTEL (WETHERSPOONS)

Tom Crudd was an eighteenth-century servant – a boot boy – at the Unicorn Hotel, then Ripon's premier hostelry, where coaches for Leeds, London and Newcastle changed horses, as did scores of private carriages. Passengers would be entertained by 'Old Boots', who, as well as offering a bootjack and slippers, would hold a coin, which he kept between his nose and chin for their amusement and his enrichment.

13. SAINSBURY'S SITE

On the Sainsbury's site in the eighteenth century stood the White Hart Inn, renamed the New Inn, the Crown & Anchor, the Crown and by 1907 the Crown Hotel when its licence was revoked for the insanitary arrangements down this yard. It then became Croft and Blackburn's garage until 1974, then Morrisons supermarket from 1977 to 2004 and finally Sainsbury's. Stand in the entrance passage and take your mind back to this.

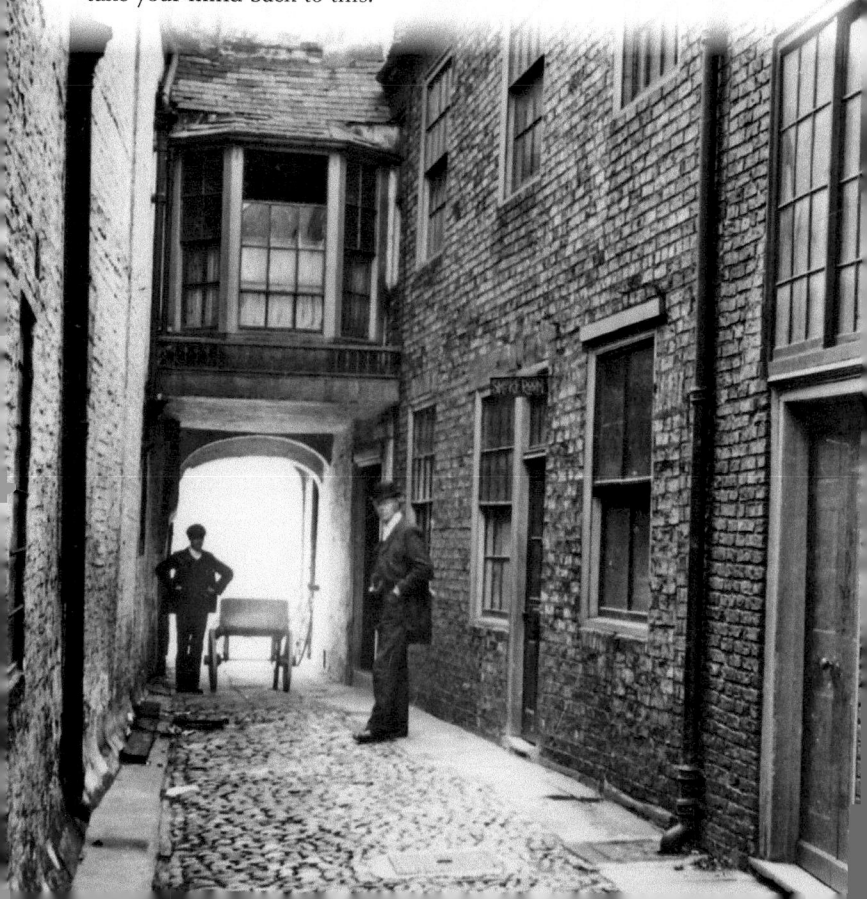

Ripon Assembly
1st Subscription Ticket
29 Oct 1801

Nº 21

(Not transferable)

14. MARKET PLACE SOUTH

Designed by James Wyatt, in 1801 the town hall was built for Mrs Allanson of Studley Royal on what had been two properties. One, an inn, was used by the Corporation for meetings. Wyatt's design included assembly rooms and a committee room. In his diary Benjamin Newton, rector of Wath from 1816 to 1818, mentions attending the Ripon Assembly, which had opened in 1801. The clock dates from 1859 and was made by Richard Blakeborough of Ripon. In medieval times the wakeman – in 1604 he became the mayor – and his officials were responsible for the running of the town. Underground toilets at the front left of the picture served the public from 1899 to 2001.

"D.P." 689-4. WESTGATE. RIPON.

15. KIRKGATE

Despite its 'Westgate' label this is Kirkgate around 1926. At one time the top part of Kirkgate was known as Duck Hill and also as Cornhill. Dating from the thirteenth century and probably earlier, Kirkgate is the traditional processional route linking the town and the minster. The Palladium cinema opened in 1916, one of three helping to provide entertainment for the thousands of soldiers based at Ripon at that time. It was the last to close, in 1982, and became a nightclub, but has been empty for several years. No. 5 Kirkgate was the town house and police station from 1836 to 1852 and 1875 to 1887.

16. KIRKGATE

A 1904 newspaper report described how children 'brought flowers and other gifts for distribution amongst the sick, poor and children's hospitals. Sunday school banners were processed along Allhallowgate, Finkle Street, Queen Street, via the Market Place and Kirkgate to the cathedral.' That year almost 600 pupils and teachers took part. From the ringing of the Pancake Bell on Shrove Tuesday, in 1998 Dean John Methuen inaugurated a new tradition of pancake races from the cathedral to the Market Place.

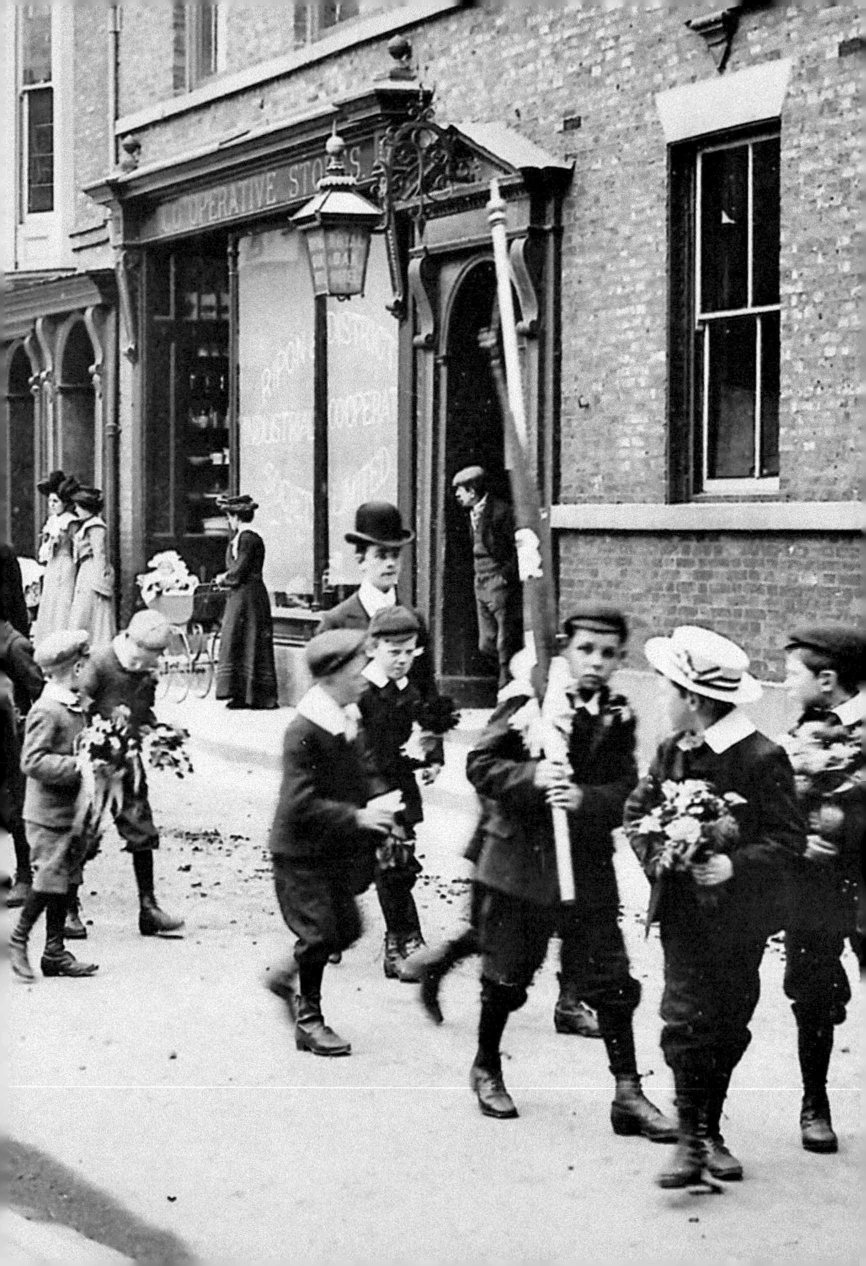
OPERATIVE

hope you will have a happy new
year. All these P.Cards are what I
take myself. The one I have

17. KIRKGATE

Although Ripon was not a gated town, a gateway, which had several rooms above, appears at the end of Kirkgate in an eighteenth-century drawing by Turner. That was to the churchyard and formed one of the sanctuary boundaries. Kirkgate is the one street left in Ripon retaining its medieval appearance. The medieval archway to the left, further along Kirkgate, led to the archbishop's palace and court and the canons' court and prison. In the 1850s Lewis Carroll not only lodged at the Unicorn but also twice with Mrs Barker at No. 32 and also with Burnett, the dean's verger, at the last house on the right, which has since been demolished.

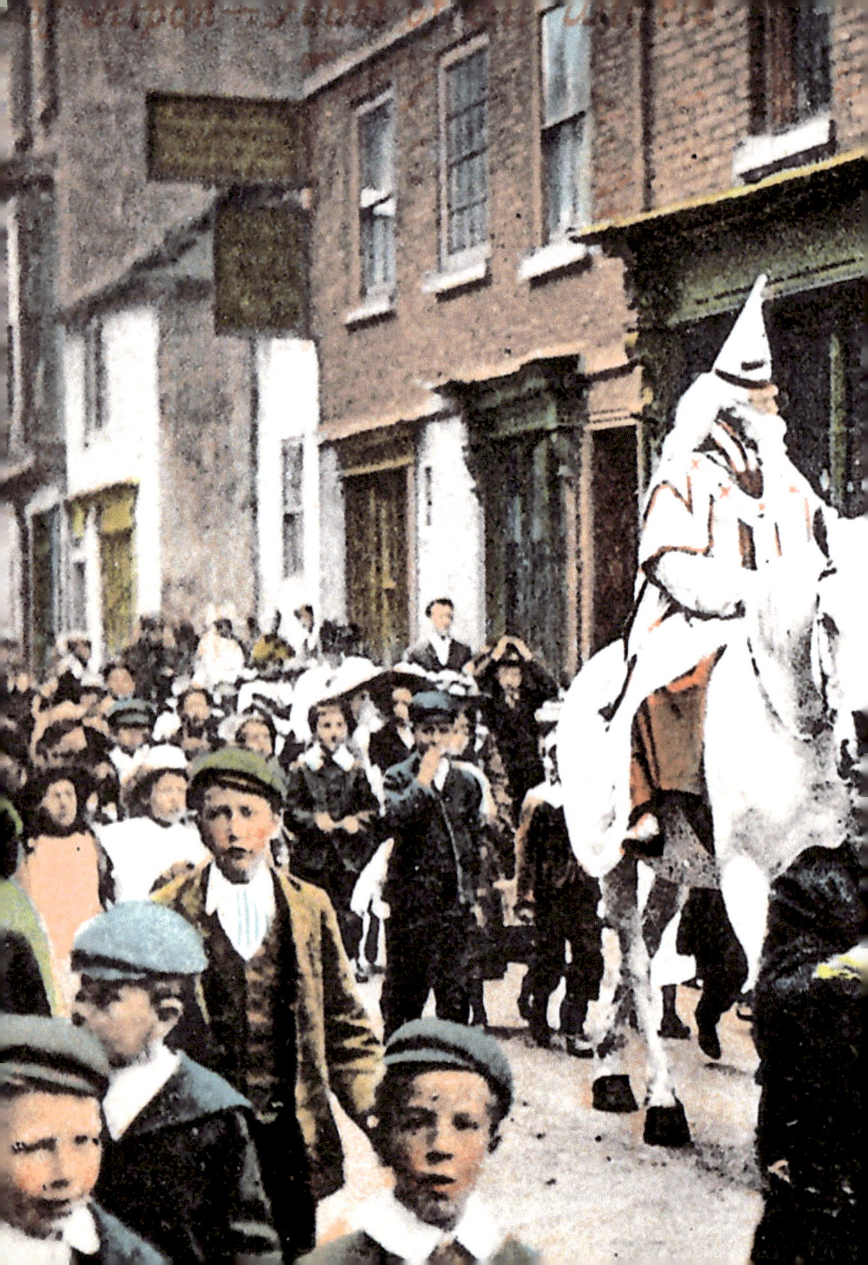

18. KIRKGATE

From the thirteenth century in April, August and October St Wilfrid's shrine would be carried down the street, the predecessor of today's Wilfrid processions. With the shrine destroyed during the Reformation, the procession was reintroduced with an effigy in the 1830s and a live figure from the mid-1840s. Medieval processions included the sanctuary men carrying their white staffs and penitents, some on their way to be beaten or whipped at the church.

Ripon Cathedral. West Front.

19. RIPON CATHEDRAL WEST FRONT

The cathedral environs and land to its north formed part of the seventh-century monastery of St Wilfrid. His great abbey church stood on the site of the present cathedral, with the crypt surviving. The very fine west front can be dated from indulgences of 1233 and 1258 to the best period of Early English architecture. In the thirteenth/fourteenth century clergy sentenced to be 'degraded' (defrocked) would be paraded to the west door where the sentence would be carried out. Notice that the top three lancets are now above the roofline. The 110-foot towers were crowned with timber spires until they were removed in 1664. The door has '1673' in nails. Pinnacles were added in 1797 and removed around 1940. The clock was raised in 1906.

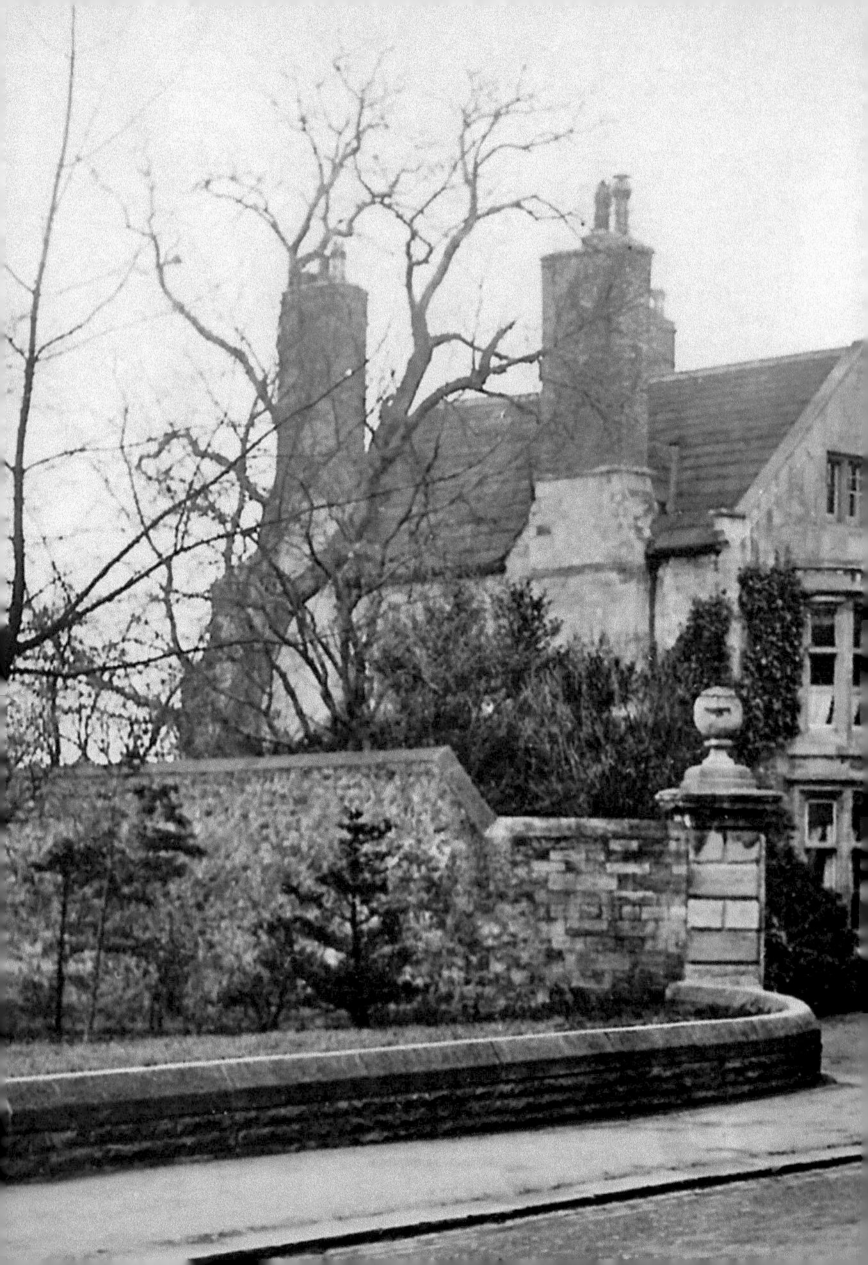

20. THE OLD DEANERY

From the seventh century St Wilfrid's monastery occupied the area to the north of the cathedral. In the fifteenth century the Bedern (College of Vicars-Choral) stood here, replacing an earlier building on Bedern Bank. After a new charter was granted to the minster in 1604, this fine limestone building was erected for the canon-in-residence. In practice it was occupied by the dean. The seventh-century Ripon Jewel, which can be seen in the cathedral, was discovered in the grounds in 1977.

Across the green is the old magistrates' court, used from 1830 to 1998. Close by stands the medieval ecclesiastical courts and prison.

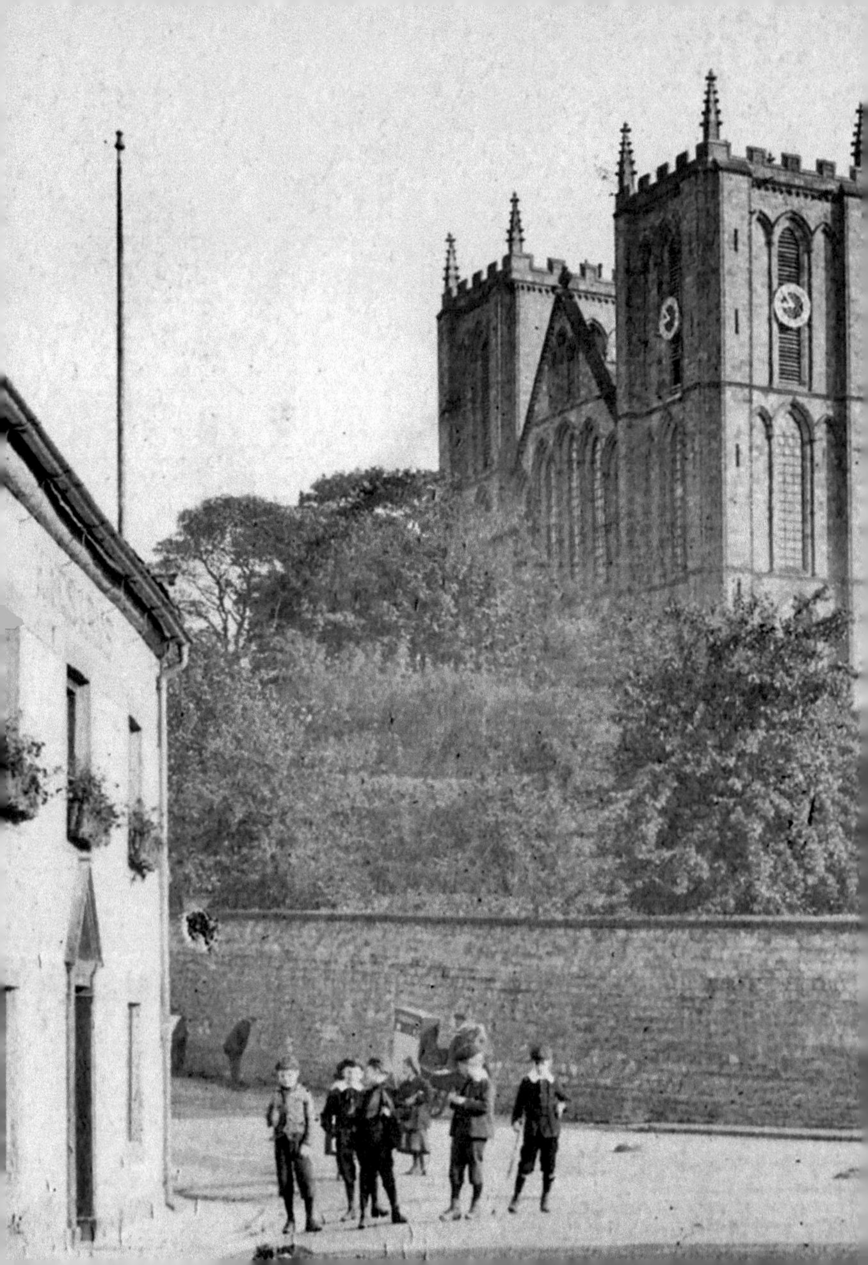

21. THE CATHEDRAL FROM BEDERN BANK

Originally 'le Walkmilnebank', from the walk or fulling mill at the bottom, in 1303 the Archbishop of York decreed that the vicars should have permanent, paid appointments and live communally in a bedern (or prayer house) so the street name changed, although in just over a hundred years the vicars had moved. At the bottom left of the picture is the Kings Arms, one of Ripon's earliest inns, which was demolished by 1959.

1434 Ripon Cathedral

22. BONDGATE GREEN BRIDGE

Archer Bridge, from the eighteenth century called Chain Bridge, was rebuilt in 1717 and replaced in 1754 by a stone footbridge, which was itself replaced in 1810–12 by the existing Bondgate Green Bridge. One of the land arches forms part of the cellar of the band room. In the fourteenth century Thorpe Prebend House was uninhabitable and being used for casting bells, but by the mid-sixteenth century it was the home of Marmaduke Bradley, last abbot of Fountains Abbey, timbers in the east wing having been felled in the winter of 1516/17. It was rebuilt around 1609 (central and west wing timbers have been dated to 1593/4) and in 1617 James I visited. In the 1890s it was converted into five cottages, then in 1913/14 gifted to the city for a museum, which closed in September 1956. Assisted by grants, the cathedral restored the building as an Interpretation Centre in 2002, which only survived a few years.

The left inset view shows the band room, tucked between Thorpe Prebend House and St Anne's, as a single-storey structure. Around 1890, with Thorpe Prebend, James Wright, plumber, bought it as a workshop and added the upper storey – scratched into an upper window is 'Thomas Wright, plumber, 1889'. In 1919 the council leased to the City Band 'the first floor of the warehouse adjoining the City Museum as a rehearsal room at a nominal rent of £2 per annum'.

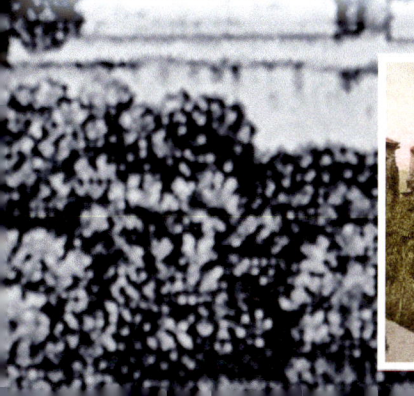

RUINS St. ANNE'S CHAPEL, RIPON

23. HIGH ST AGNESGATE/ST ANNE'S HOSPITAL CHAPEL

By the old Archer Bridge, the smallest of the hospital chapels offered 'hospitality' in two dormitories, each with four beds plus two common beds and a resident chaplain. Annusgate is mentioned in 1228 and Agnesgate in 1462. The earliest documentary evidence for St Anne's is from 1438, but parts of the building are considered earlier. The nave was demolished in 1869 when the almshouses were built, with the Greenwood family as major benefactors. The trust was reorganised in 1884. Restoration of the almshouses took place in the 1970s and during the 1980s the accommodation was upgraded.

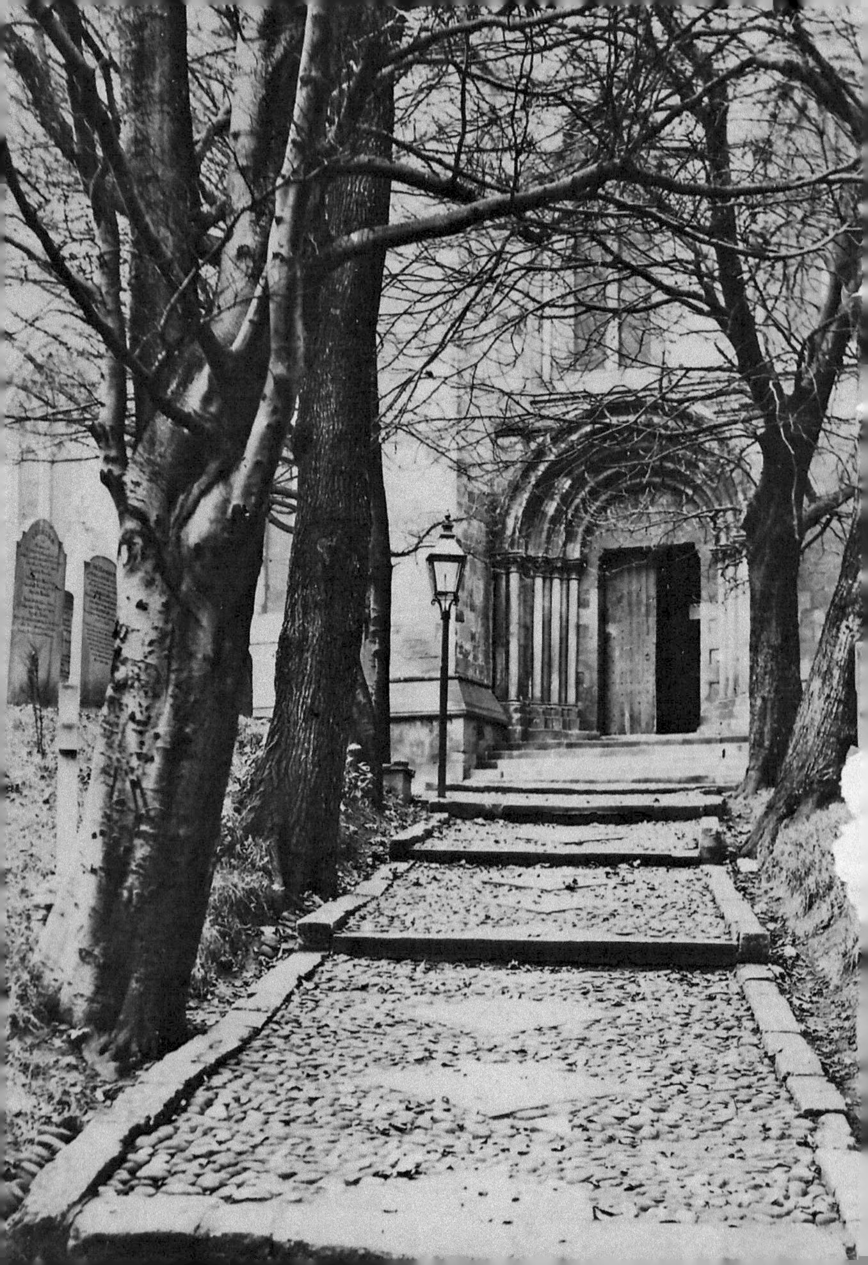

24. RIPON CATHEDRAL SOUTH WALK

The very elaborate south doorway of the largely late twelfth-century transept was once covered by a Renaissance porch of four orders, the uppermost of its five shafts projecting considerably, two uncommonly sharing one abacus. The foliage on the capitals is almost Early English in style. To the left of the arch is a modern replacement mass dial. It is said that those engaged in trade would use this door while the gentry used the west doors.

In the medieval period outside the churchyard wall to the left stood the house of the prebendary (canon) of either Stanwick or possibly Monkton. The current early Georgian house has associations with Lewis Carroll, whose father served as a canon of the cathedral. To the right, until 1894, stood the grammar school.

Ripon Cathedral from River

25. ALMA WEIR AND FOOTBRIDGE

Although the present structure dates from 1984, a weir is shown here around 1800, but it is possible that a dam fed a pre-Conquest mill downstream at Low Mill. A wooden footbridge was first built in 1862. The name Alma commemorates the Crimean War. An enthusiastic collector of Crimean War memorabilia lived at Alma House (from 1877 to 1927 Skellfield School), the building to the left as you approach the footbridge. Successive rebuilds of the bridge show two, three or four rails. Skellfield Terrace was built in three phases by 1905 – compare the variations in the roof slates.

V. & S., Ltd.. D.

Harrison's Serie

26. CANAL BASIN

Ripon Canal was built between 1767 and 1773. Linking Ripon to the navigable stretches of the Ure, it took bricks, lead, butter, cheese, corn and agricultural produce and returned with coal. In debt by 1820, it was eventually bought by the Leeds & Thirsk Railway. In 1947 it was declared a 'remainder waterway' and in 1955 the locks were blown in. The waterway was restored from 1982 to 1997, largely through the efforts of the Ripon Canal Society. Development round the basin began in 1999.

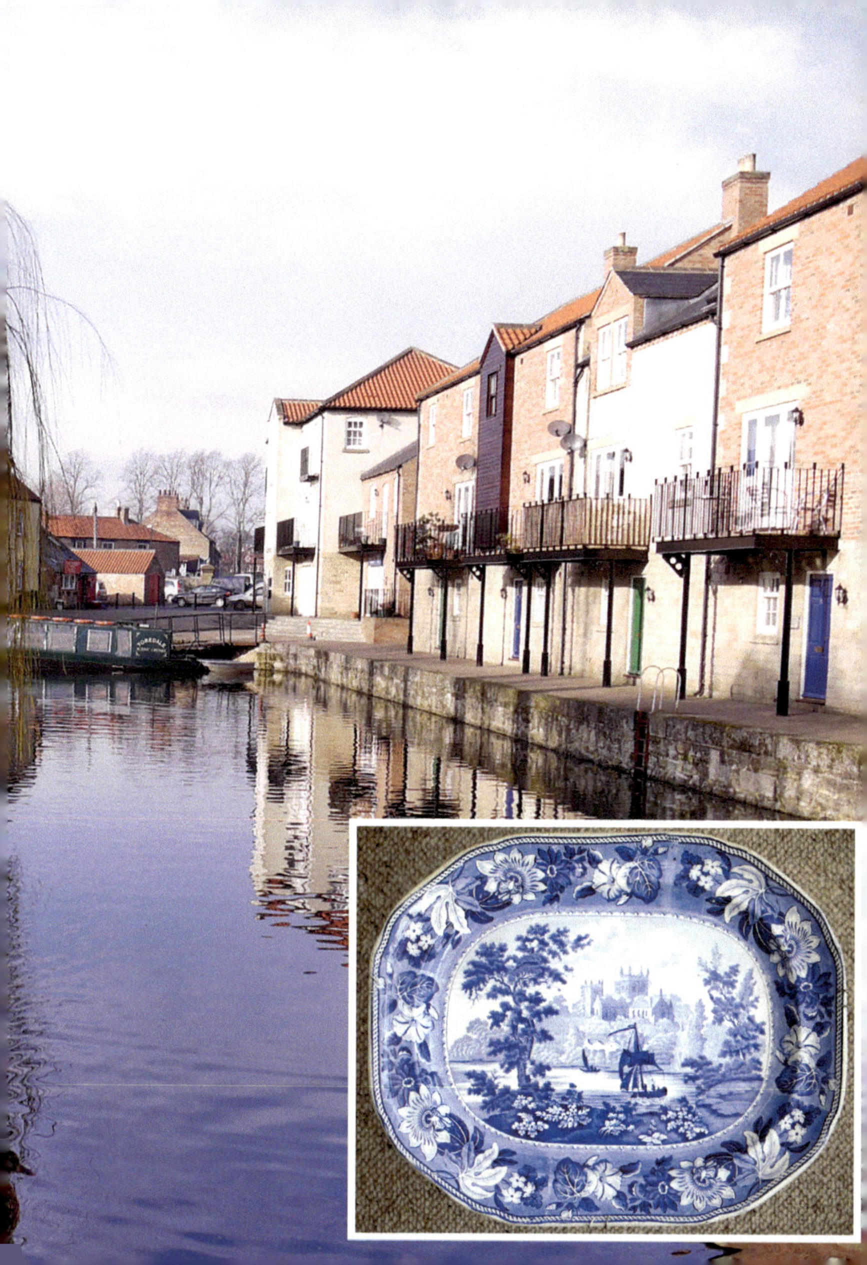

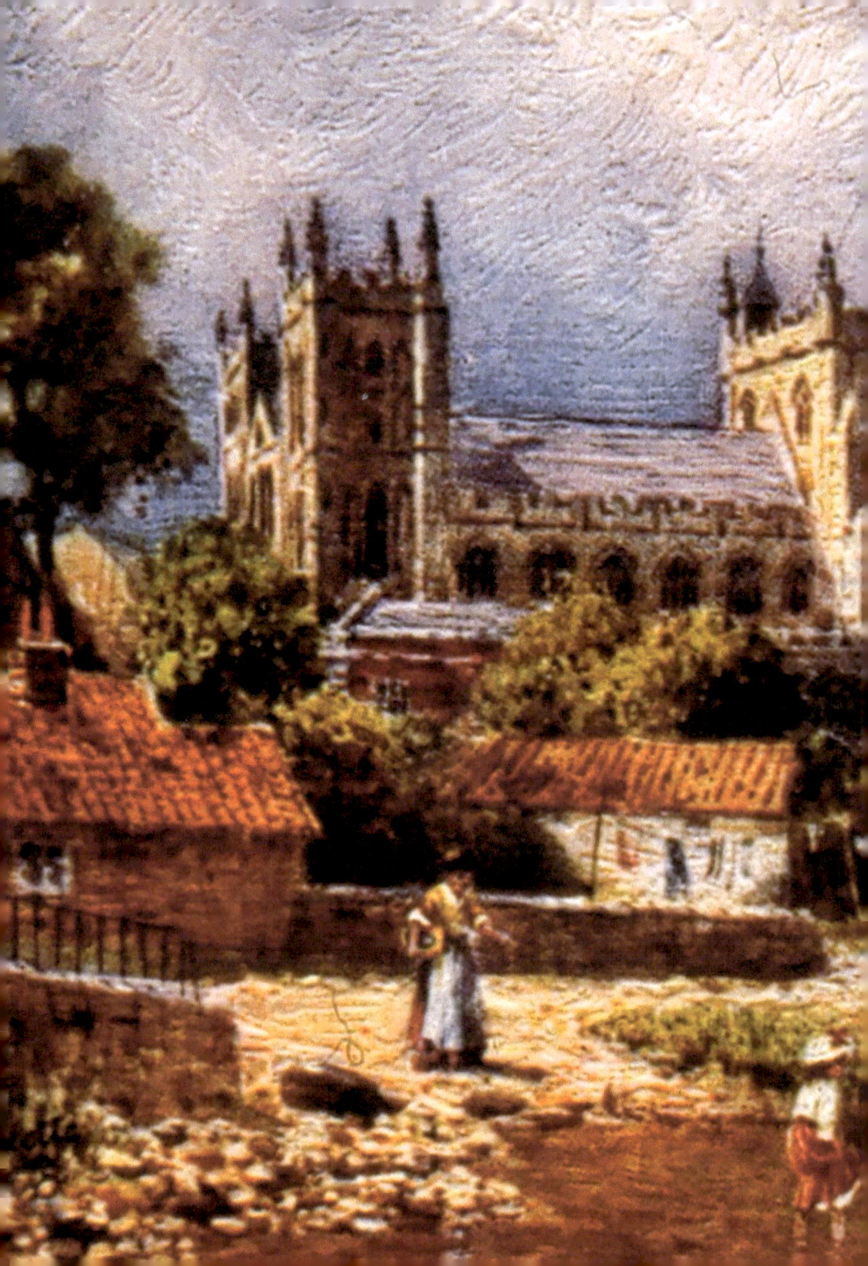

27. MILL FIELD PLAY PARK

On the south bank around 40 metres upstream from Bondgate Green Bridge a low weir directs water through a grill to feed the canal. After a weir for Low Mill was built downstream the mill race re-entered the river opposite. The present culvert is modern. There was once a fulling mill, which was long gone by 1643 when it was referred to as New Mill, a corn mill. Rebuilt later, it operated under a co-operative as Union Mill. Having lost its water supply in 1892, it was demolished in 1915 and the site was given to the city by the church as a children's play park.

From the early twelfth century the River Skell was bridged into Bondgate, with the chapel of St John the Baptist nearby. The present bridge dates from 1892 and the chapel from the 1860s.

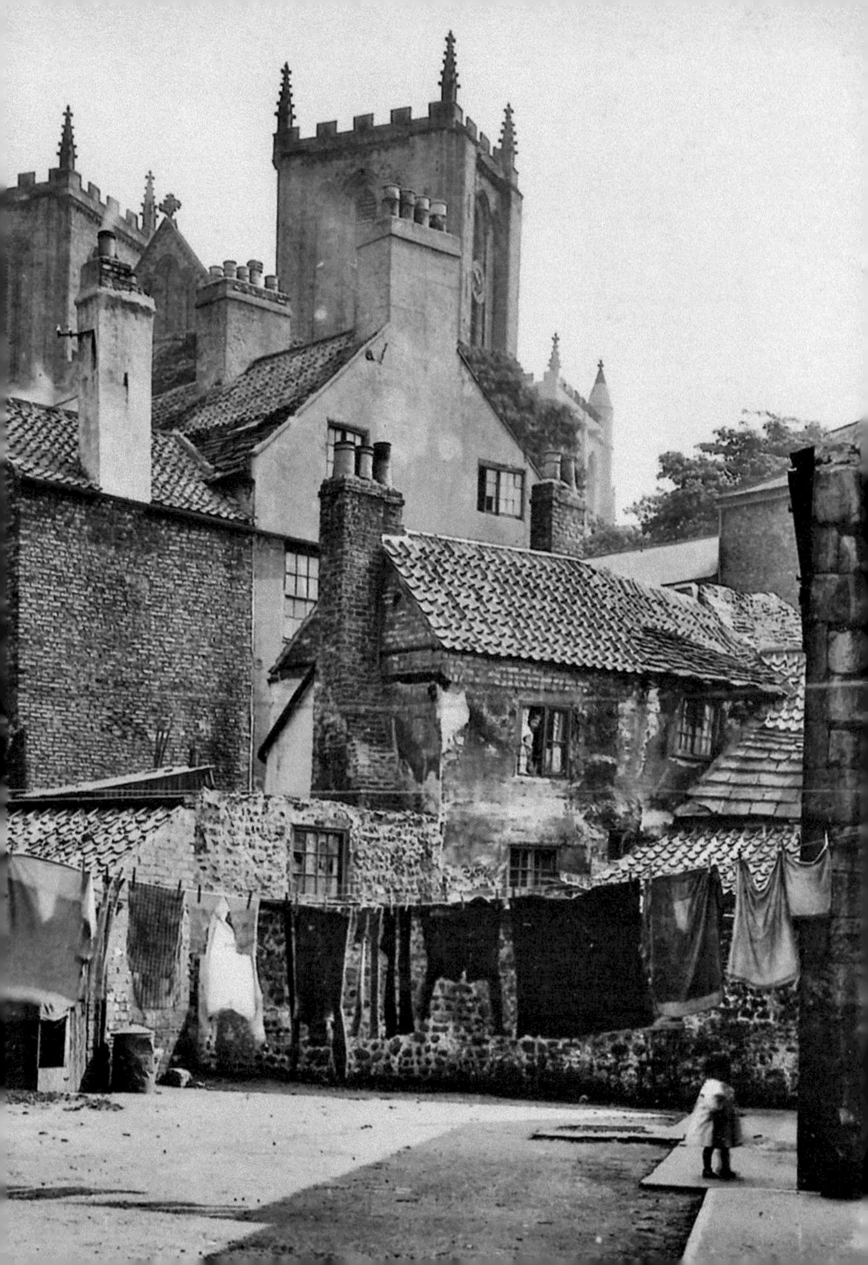

28. RIPON CATHEDRAL FROM YORK YARD

This view would now be described as from Bedern Court. Possibly as early as the twelfth century, the mill race continued past Duck Hill Mill along Millgate (Skellgarths), making the road so narrow that by the 1830s the mill race here was the earliest to be covered over. In 1959 the site was cleared to be used to store fairground equipment, when it became part of Doubtfire's Yard. Prior to rebuilding, in 1995 evidence of an oxbow lake was found here together with lime pits from the tanning industry. A little further along, from the early nineteenth century, Ingram's Kirkgate foundry stood at the foot of Peacock's Passage. The milepost near the entrance to Ripley is their work.

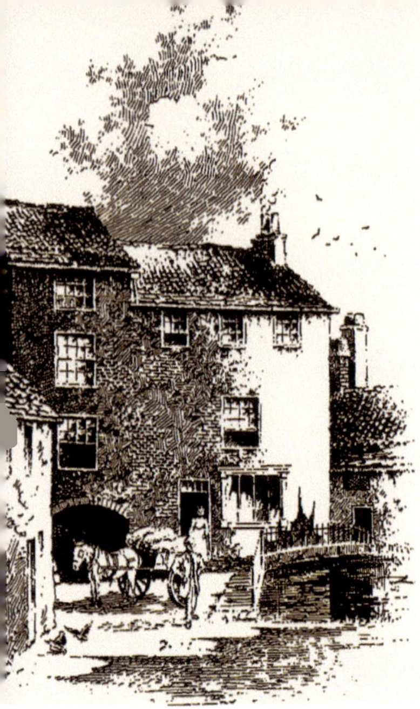

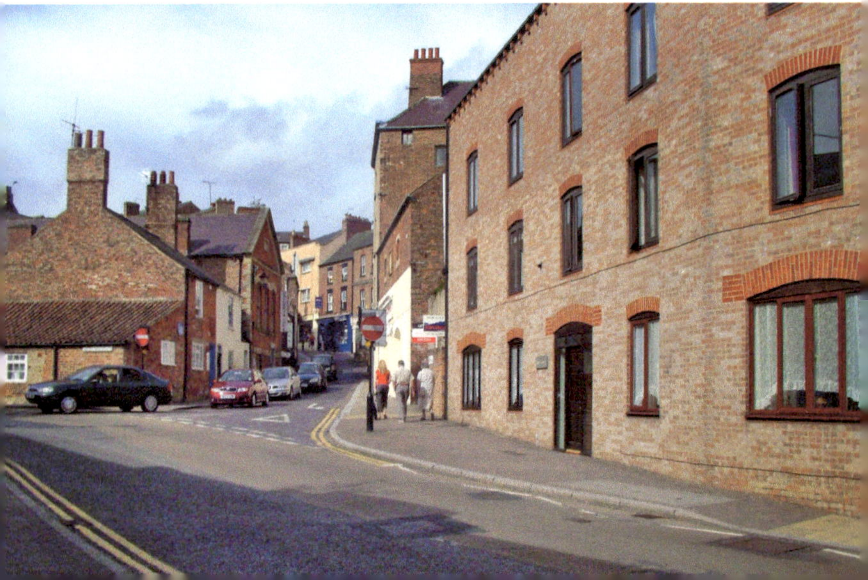

29. DUCK HILL MILL

At the foot of Duck Hill stood Bymill, the town mill, thought to be the second earliest of Ripon's medieval mills. It drew its water from an exceptionally long mill stream starting near the confluence of the rivers Laver and Skell (High Cleugh). The bridge was essential as the millpond almost filled the road, the ducks giving the hill its name. In the medieval period in the area between the mill race and the river Ripon's cloth workers could be found. Inspectors were appointed to try to keep the waters clean as the mill race also provided the town's drinking water. In the eighteenth century, when owned by Ald. Askwith of the Royal Oak, the mill pumped water up to the Market Place. After the collapse of High Cleugh dam in 1892 part of its site was sold for road widening. A steam engine drove the wheel producing animal feeds until 1957, when the mill was put up for auction but withdrawn. In 1988 it was converted into dwellings.

30. WATER SKELLGATE

High Skellgate appears as Over Skelgate in 1467, which with Water Skellgate and Skellgarths indicates the route of the Skell through the town. The mill race crossed Borrage Green Common (remains can be found in the gardens of Mallorie Park Drive), 9 feet wide and 12 feet deep, to Low Mill. In later centuries the water returned to the river near Bondgate Green Bridge. Water Skellgate was culverted in 1875.

Starting life as the Public Rooms in 1832, Lewis Carroll records attending a concert here in 1850, which was rebuilt in 1885 to seat 1,000. After renovation it reopened in 1908 as the Victoria Hall/Opera House and has served variously as a roller-skating rink, cinema, bingo hall and function room. In 1976 it was gutted by fire and is currently an antiques centre. This card is postmarked 4 September 1915.

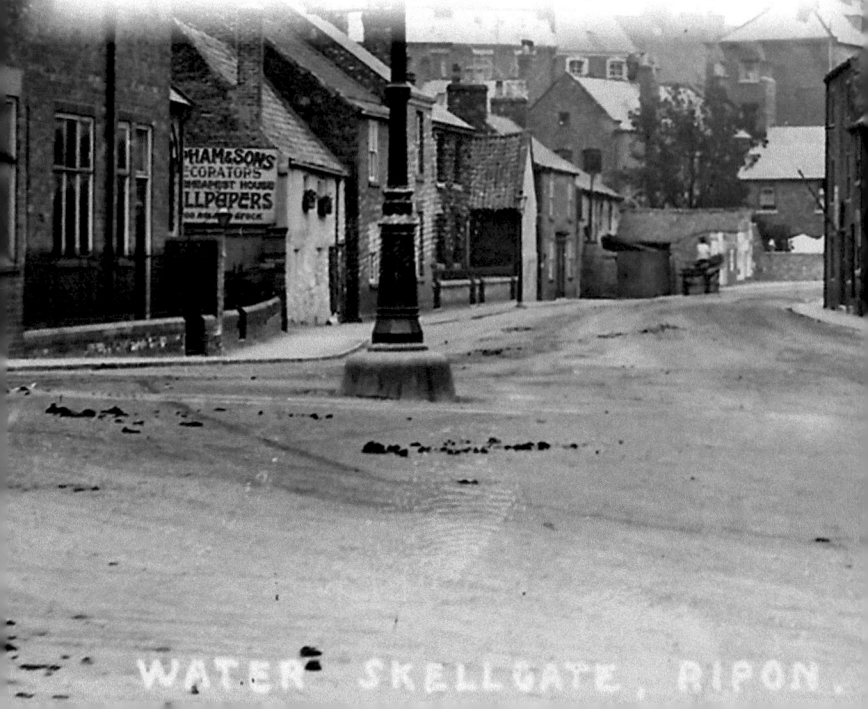

BAYLEYS SERIES.

31. LOW SKELLGATE

Low Skellgate led to Borrage Green, common land where cattle were pastured, and is first mentioned in the thirteenth century. Because of its narrowness the street has suffered from heavy traffic and businesses have found it hard to survive. The Turk's Head pub closed around ten years ago. From 1796 New Connection Wesleyans had a chapel in Turk's Head Yard until 1860 when they moved to the Zion Chapel in Blossomgate. In a warehouse in Heath's Court in the nineteenth century Roman Catholics celebrated Mass here until St Wilfrid's Church was built.

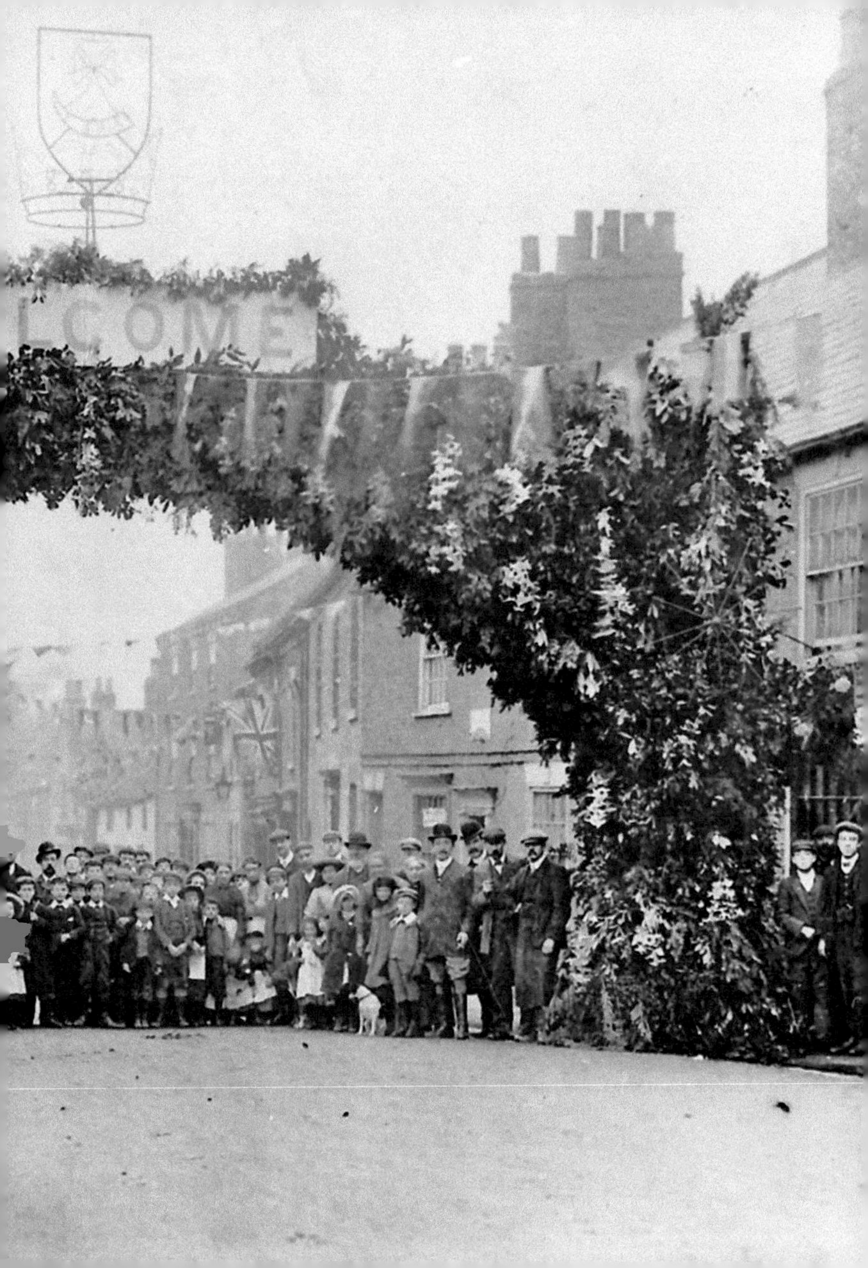
LCOME

RIVER SKELL, Near CAMP.

32. WILLIAMSON PAINT WORKS AND RIVER SKELL

Daniel Williamson befriended a Huguenot refugee who had found his way to Ripon. In return Williamson was to learn the secrets of varnish making, establishing a new industry in Ripon in 1775, eventually creating the first 'city of varnish' in the country. The site near Borrage Bridge, previously Skin Yard, was acquired in the twentieth century; their earlier works were further downstream. They moved to Stonebridgegate in 1985.

33. BORRAGE BRIDGE

By the 1530s there was a stone bridge here, possibly the one identified in fourteenth-century wills as Esgatebrigg. Being the first bridge over the river after it entered the town, the name possibly derives from 'Skell'. Borrage derives from 'burgage' – the bridge gave the burgesses access to their grazing rights at the far side of Borrage Green. Traditionally the cloth workers were concentrated between Borrage and Bondgate bridges, until Ripon lost its position as a leading Yorkshire cloth town in the fifteenth century. Barefoot Street comes from 'bere-ford' ('barley-ford'). The bridge was rebuilt in 1765 and widened in 1886. The join is visible underneath.

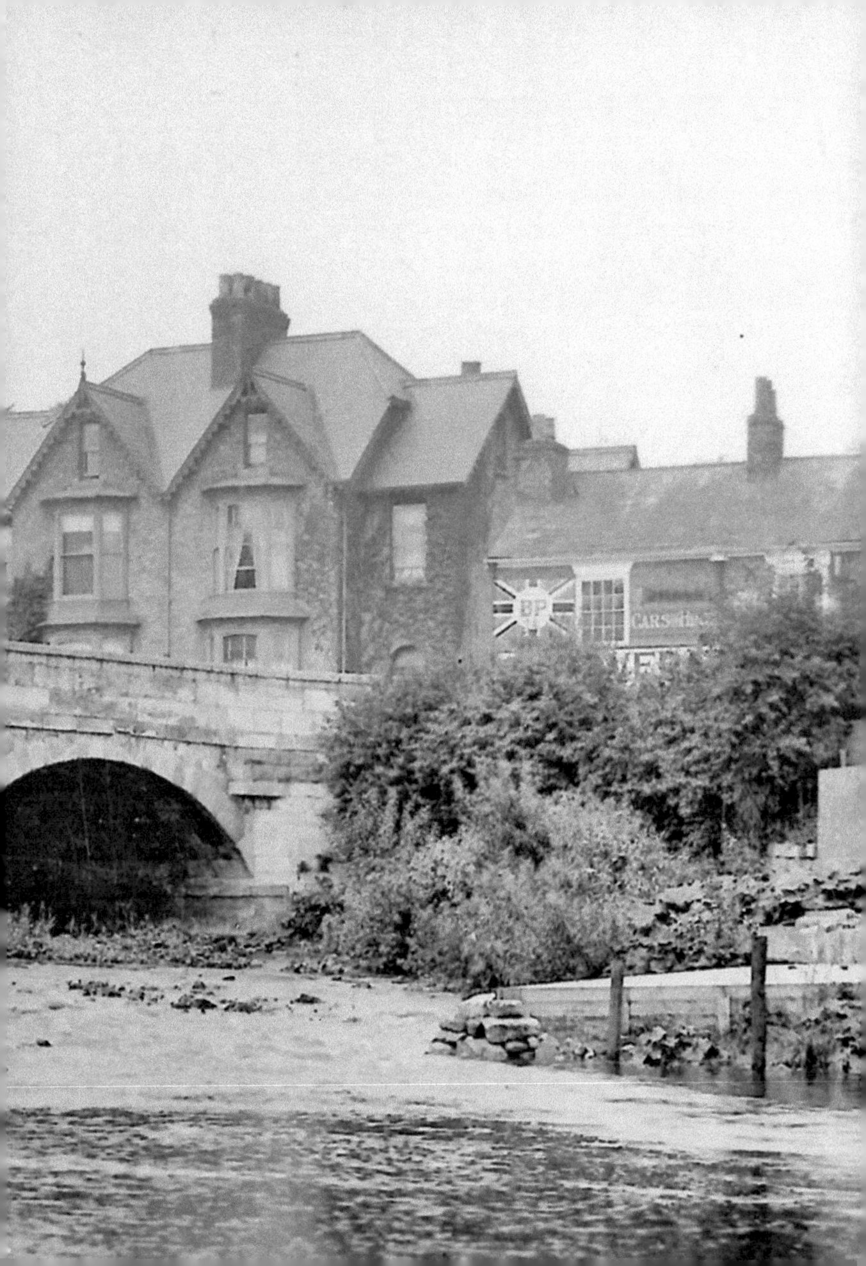
BP
CARS

34. RUSTIC BRIDGE

In September 1898 a new wooden bridge of intertwined branches, Rustic Bridge, also known as Willows Bridge, was built over the confluence of the Laver and the Skell to Borrage Lane. During the First World War soldiers used it between the army camps and town. Often at risk from floods, it was heavily damaged in August 1927. Later it appeared in metal until the early 1980s when it was replaced by timber.

Ripon Cathedral, from Banks of Skell.

FAIRY STEPS, BORRAGE GLEN, RIPON. (9)

35. FAIRY STEPS

A little further upstream, the steps are sometimes said to have first appeared during the First World War but 'man-size' steps show at this point on earlier postcards. In the absence of other evidence it is suggested that it was during First World War training the side slopes were added to take the wheels of gun carts with the shallow (fairy) steps to assist the mules as they hauled the carts up the bank.

36. HIGH CLEUGH

The weir on the bend on the River Laver had already been washed away three times in the century when, in 1892, it collapsed, never to be replaced, closing down several corn mills as its now waterless mill stream passed through Ripon. In 1919 a scheme was drawn up to construct a miniature lake at High Cleugh, but the city council declined to pay the £20 for materials. Stakes from the dam were still visible in 1948 when Riponians were getting used to the new concrete embankments and breakwaters.

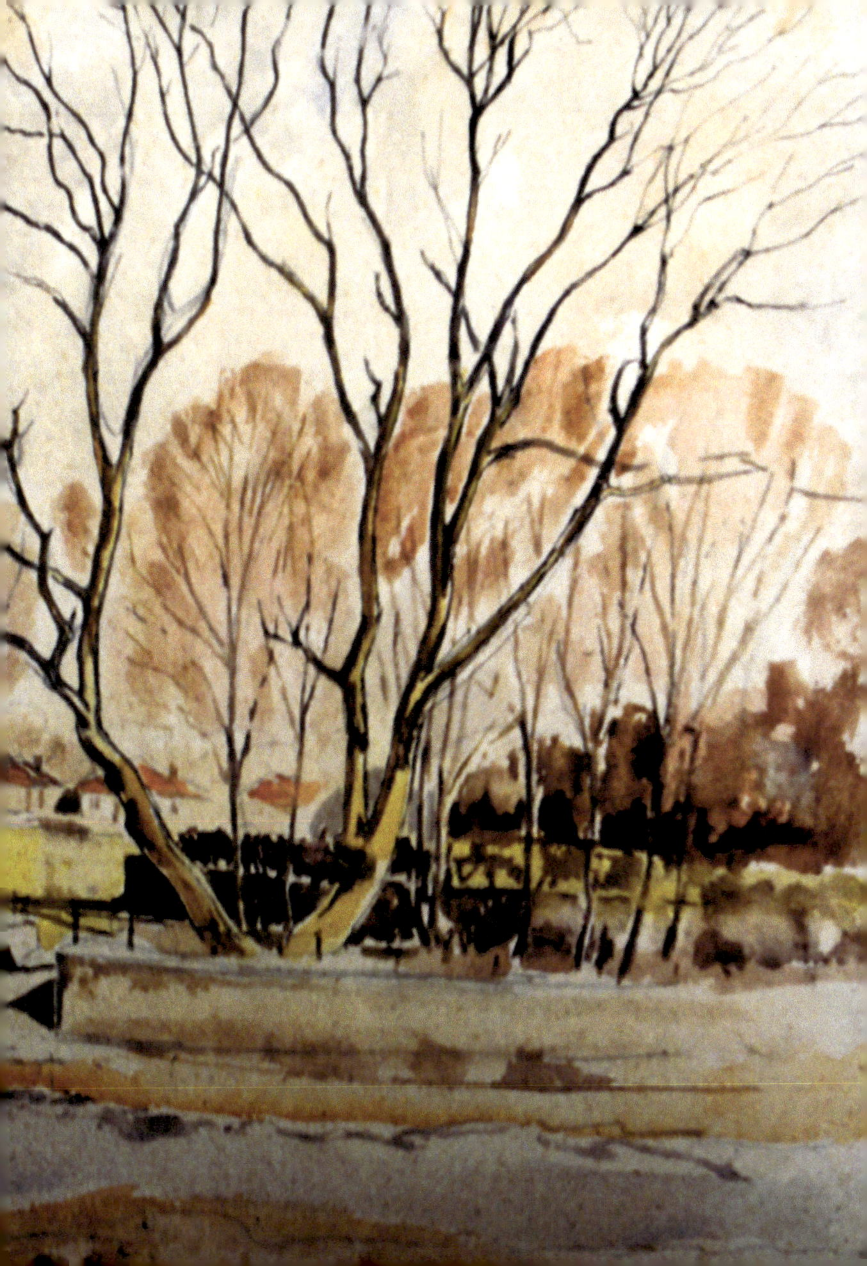

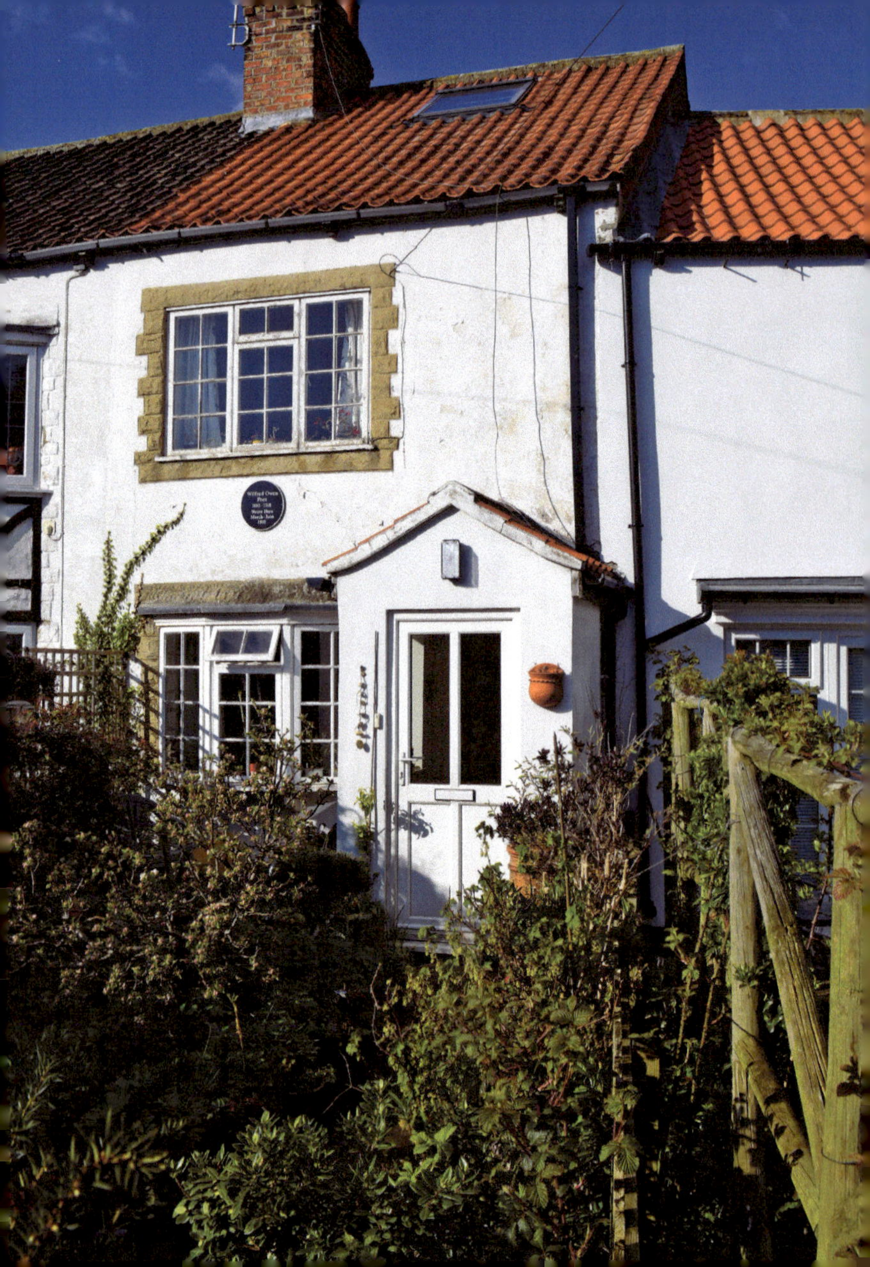
Wilfred Owen
Poet

37. BORRAGE LANE

Wilfred Owen is one of the most important poets of the First World War. He came to the army camp in Ripon – 'an awful camp' – in March 1918 following a period of treatment for shell shock. As he had done elsewhere, he rented rooms at No. 7 Borrage Lane (now No. 24) to work on his poetry when off-duty. Here Owen worked on some of his most famous poems including 'Futility', 'Mental Cases', 'The Send-off' and possibly 'Strange Meeting'. These powerful works expose the horror and tragedy of war, mourning the loss of so many lives.

> All a poet can do today is warn.
> My subject is War, and the pity of War.
> The Poetry is in the pity.

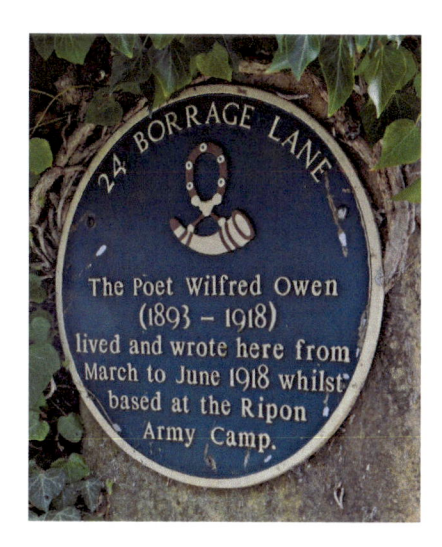

Old Westgate, Ripon.

38. WESTGATE

The street led westwards to Bishopton Bridge via Blossomgate before High Westgate (Park Street) was developed in the late seventeenth century. It is one of Ripon's earliest streets, recorded from 1228 when most of it belonged to the minster canons. In 1458 Westgate butcher Robert Morton and five others were sentenced to be beaten on four separate occasions for failing to carry their sanctuary rods in public. One was pardoned for his age and weakness of mind.

From 1903 street widening took place before coming to a sudden halt outside No. 5, then Dr Collier's house. Country folk coming to the town on market day could tie up their horses for the day. Signs for the Green Dragon and the Queen Alexandra can be seen, with the Slip Inn at No. 7 and the Black Swan and the Black Horse further down opposite, with the eighteenth-century theatre beyond.

39. SPA BATHS

This card is postmarked August 1906. In 1905 the new Spa Baths opened, the ornate interior of the pump room finished with tile, marble and stained glass. The baths were open from 7 a.m. to 7 p.m. Admission and a glass of sulphur water cost one penny each. As elsewhere, the spa declined in the interwar years and in 1936, after many years of waiting, a public swimming pool was incorporated into the building.

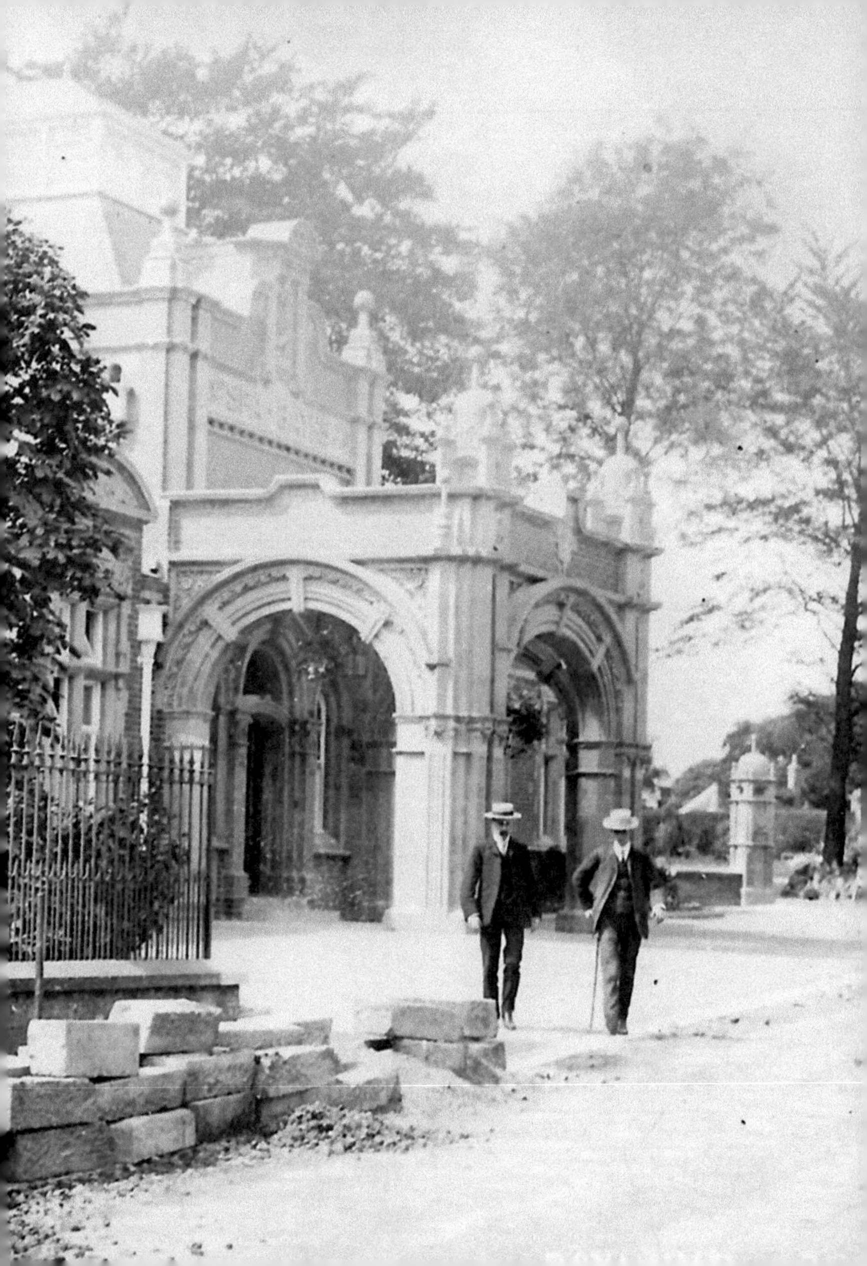

40. SPA GARDENS

Inside the Spa Gardens, in May 1912 a statue of the 1st Marquis of Ripon (1827–1909) was unveiled. Born at No. 10 Downing Street, he went on to a distinguished career with the Liberal Party, holding many high offices but still finding time to become Mayor of Ripon (1895–96) and taking an interest in local affairs, especially education. The war memorial was erected in 1921 and lists 260 names from the First World War.

Spa Gardens, Ripon.

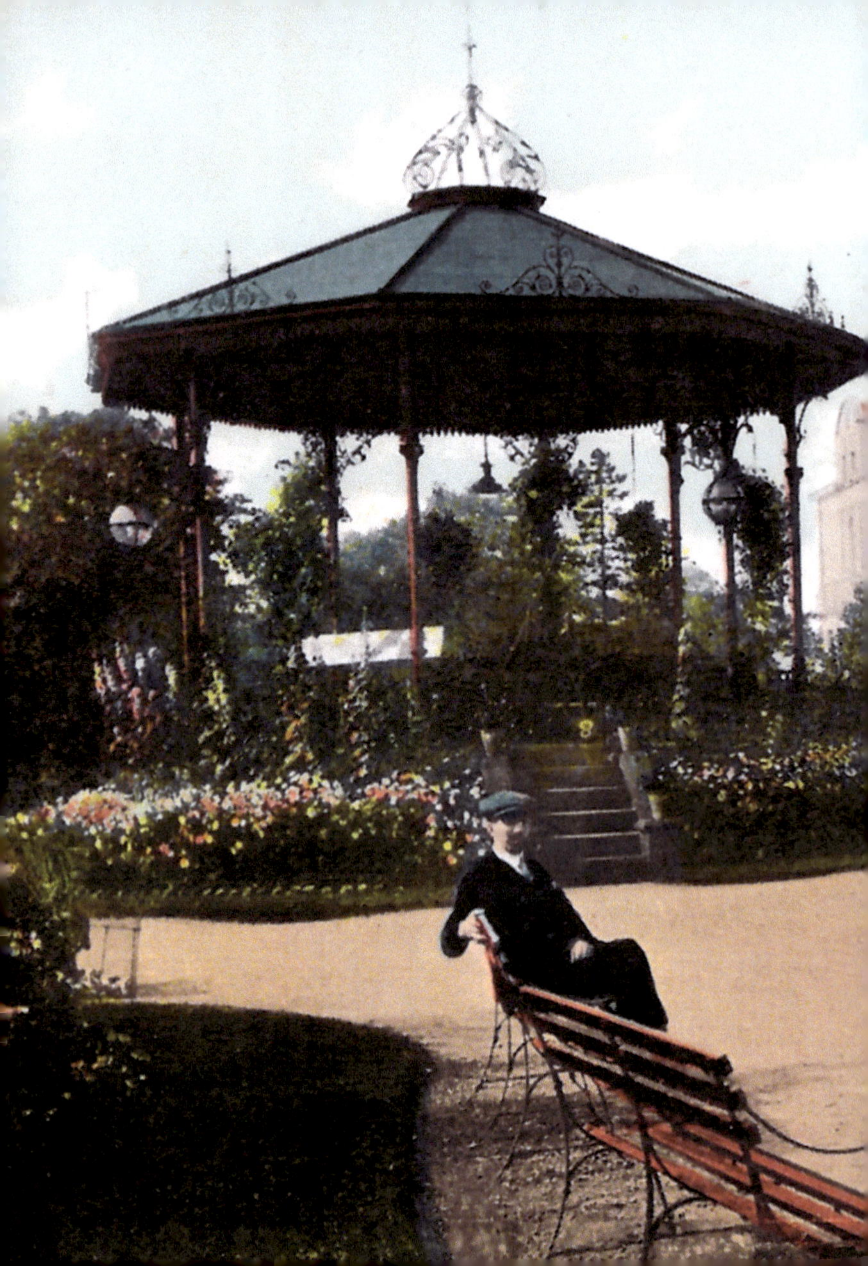

41. SPA GARDENS BANDSTAND AND SPA HOTEL

The link between taking the waters and taking fresh air and exercise was once strongly emphasised, so in 1900 the Marquis of Ripon sold the former drill field for a pump room and spa. The gardens were laid out in 1902. The bandstand followed a year later and, against much opposition, Sunday concerts were presented from 1905. The creation of the spa was an attempt to raise Ripon's depressed economy in the first decade of the twentieth century and to generate a demand for accommodation. To that end the Spa Hydro (now Hotel) opened in 1909. The croquet lawns host national competitions.

Ripon Spa. Gardens and Hydro.

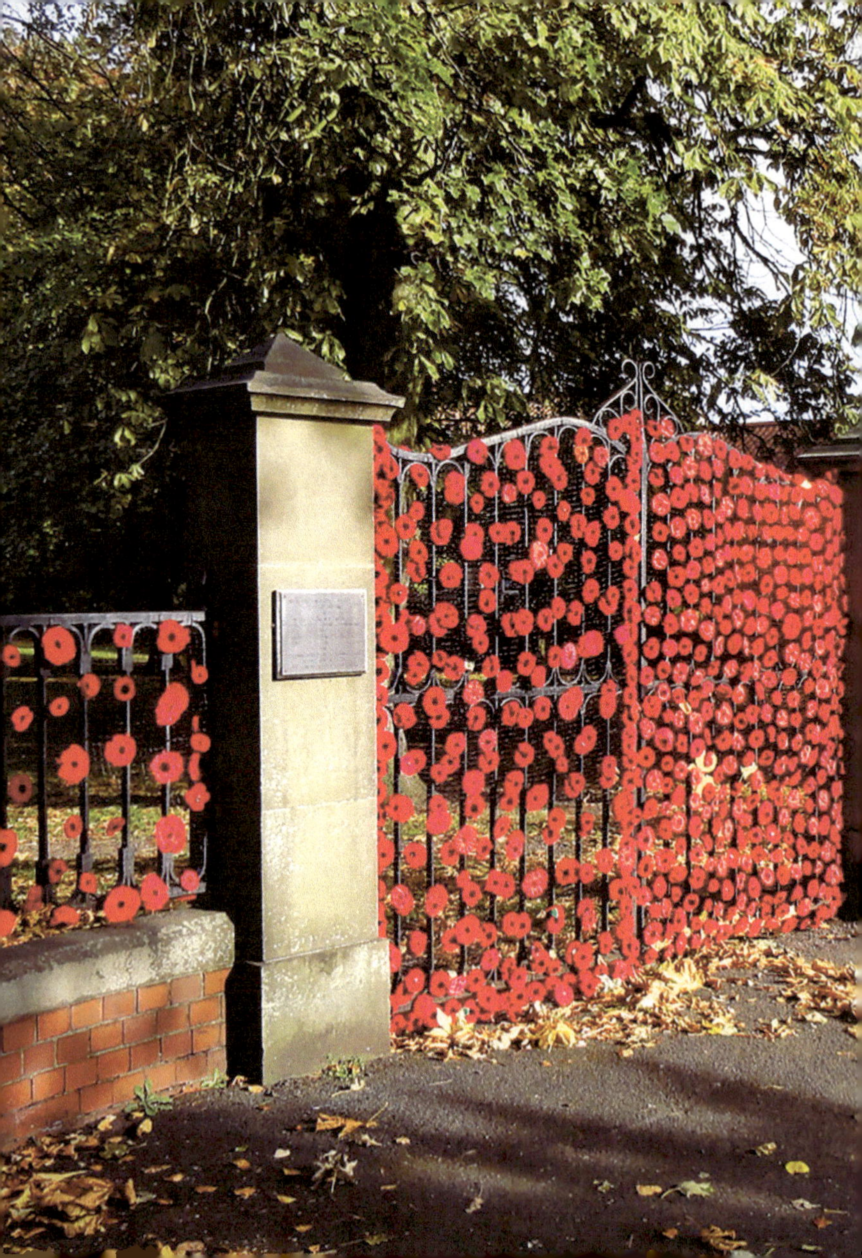

42. SPA PARK

In June 1923 two small fields, now Spa Park, were bought by the city council for £1,450. The tennis courts arrived three years later, but June 1939 brought approval for air-raid trenches to be dug. The replacement gates were presented by the Royal Engineers in June 1989, commemorating the 40th anniversary of the granting of the Freedom of Ripon to the corps. The photograph here was taken in November 2018.

The Maidens Bower, or maze, had been recut (diameter 20 yards) in 1809 along the present Palace Road, but was lost to ploughing in 1827 after the enclosure of High Common. The Rotary Club created this miniature version in 2001. Enclosure of the commons meant that animals being driven to market could no longer access the river to drink, so in 1875, by North Bridge, Dr John Severs provided this fountain with troughs for animals and humans. In 1929 it was moved to Spa Park, now without its pinnacle.

Behind Holyoake Terrace note the eighteenth-century gazebos affording views across open country from the grand houses on Park Street.

43. HOLY TRINITY CHURCH

The tall, broach spire of Holy Trinity Church is one of Ripon's landmarks. Early English in style, it was built in 1826–28. Holy Trinity Church was adopted by the tradesmen as their church, particularly after the minster became the cathedral in 1836. In 1984–85 the crypt was cleared of burials and refurbished to provide social and meetings areas and in 2001 further work extended this facility.

44. ST WILFRID'S ROMAN CATHOLIC CHURCH

Joseph Hansom's St Wilfrid's Catholic Church of 1862 replaced a meeting room off Low Skellgate, used after Roman Catholics were permitted public worship following the Reformation. Until 1939 the secondary school was housed in buildings opposite the Wesleyan chapel. 'Killikrankie', the footpath opposite the Catholic church, was named after battles there between the boys of the grammar and secondary schools. It is one of the 'public foot roads' established after the enclosure of the commons.

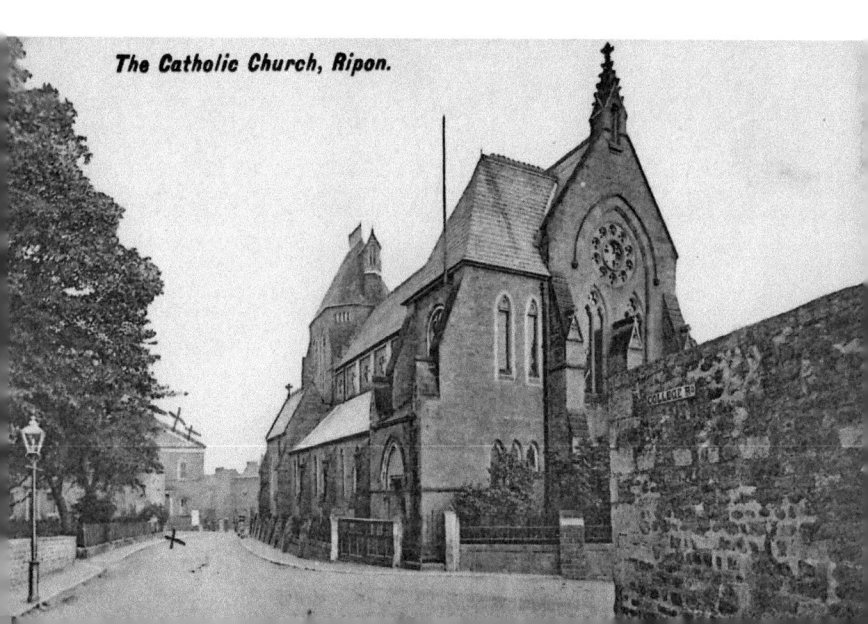

The Catholic Church, Ripon.

45. COLTSGATE HILL

In 1533 this route, leading across the open country to the ford at West Tanfield, was where the colts were tethered and it was known as Coltestakes. In 1771 it was Cowsgate Hill. The chapel, founded in 1777, was the town's first Wesleyan chapel, where Wesley himself preached in 1780. Rebuilt in a classical style in 1861 to seat 1,000 worshippers, services continued until August 1962. The junction with North Street changed dramatically with the opening of Marshall Way in 2009.

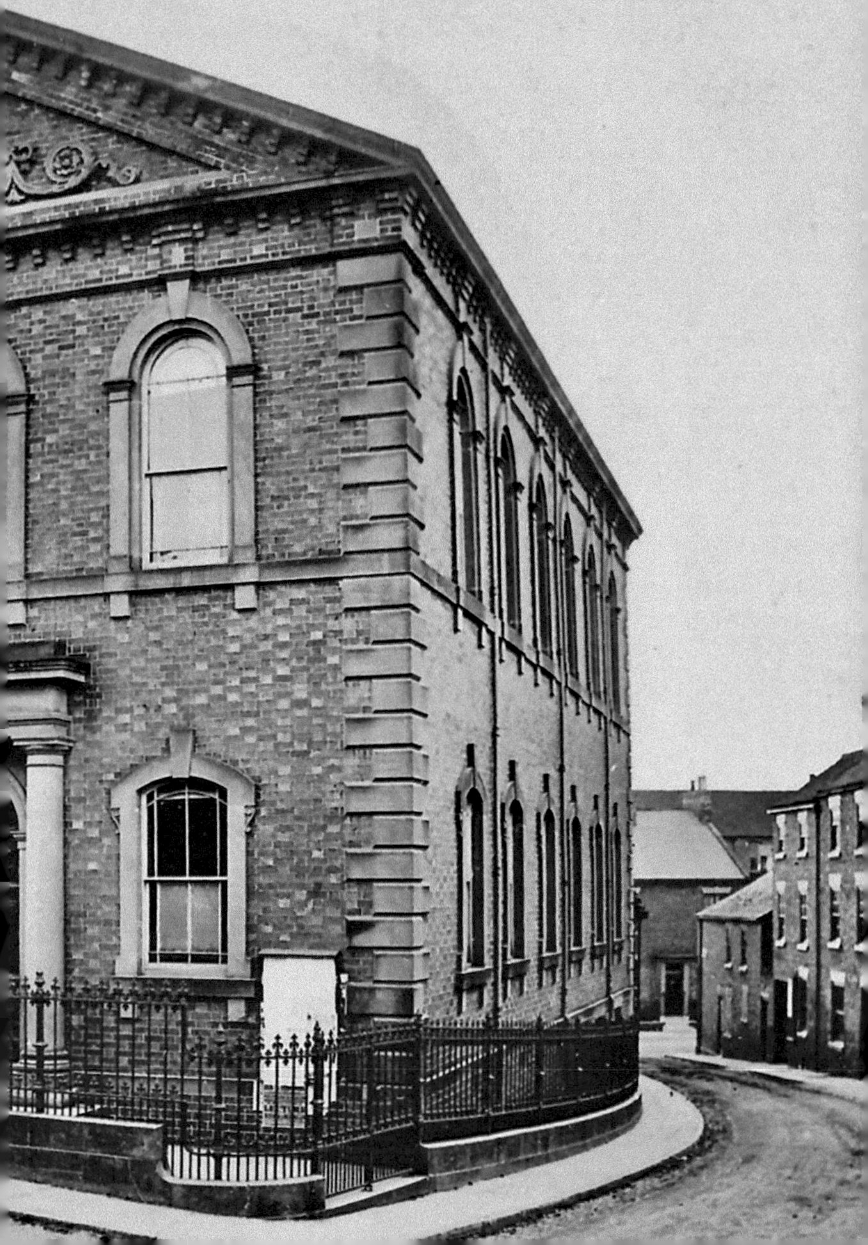

NORTH

46. NORTH STREET

North Street was called Horsefair until the nineteenth century. As part of the redevelopment following the 1870s road widening, the St Wilfrid's Hotel was built at the junction of Allhallowgate and North Street. At No. 21 stood Kearsley's foundry. Kearsley's also owned one of the paint works. For nearly a century Abbott's furniture works and showrooms stood opposite Curzon cinema.

To return to the Market Place continue along North Street or take a short diversion left along Allhallowgate to the Workhouse Museum and then along Finkle Street to the Market Place.

ABOUT THE AUTHOR

Born in Yorkshire, Maurice Taylor has lived in Ripon for nearly forty years. He has held voluntary office within Ripon with various organisations including the Civic Society and Friends of Ripon Cathedral and is a former chairman of the Dales Centre of the National Trust and the Friends of the Leper Chapel.

An interest in local history developed while attending the former Ripon Teacher Training College. Following a successful teaching career Maurice took early retirement, allowing him to concentrate on research and lecturing within his areas of interest including significant work on Lewis Carroll and the north.

He arranges the weekly Wakeman Lectures and the Ripon U3A Local History Group. Before he became severely sight impaired in 2011 he ran classes for the WEA and North Yorkshire County Council and has spoken widely to adult education and other interest groups.

In addition to conducting guided walks of his own, including the Ripon Ghost Walk for twenty-five years, he served for many years as a voluntary guide at Ripon Cathedral and Fountains Abbey and led the Historic Churches Tours for Ripon International Festival. He was heavily involved with the research during the restoration of Thorpe Prebend House as Ripon Cathedral's Interpretation Centre. He has published widely on the history of Ripon and this is his tenth book.